Library Management:
A Case Study Approach

CHANDOS
INFORMATION PROFESSIONAL SERIES

Series Editor: Ruth Rikowski
(email: Rikowskigr@aol.com)

Chandos' new series of books are aimed at the busy information professional. They have been specially commissioned to provide the reader with an authoritative view of current thinking. They are designed to provide easy-to-read and (most importantly) practical coverage of topics that are of interest to librarians and other information professionals. If you would like a full listing of current and forthcoming titles, please visit our web site **www.chandospublishing.com** or contact Hannah Grace-Williams on email info@chandospublishing.com or telephone number +44 (0) 1865 884447.

New authors: we are always pleased to receive ideas for new titles; if you would like to write a book for Chandos, please contact Dr Glyn Jones on email gjones@chandospublishing.com or telephone number +44 (0) 1865 884447.

Bulk orders: some organisations buy a number of copies of our books. If you are interested in doing this, we would be pleased to discuss a discount. Please contact Hannah Grace-Williams on email info@chandospublishing.com or telephone number +44 (0) 1865 884447.

Library Management: A Case Study Approach

EDITED BY
RAVONNE A. GREEN

Chandos Publishing
Oxford · England

Chandos Publishing (Oxford) Limited
Chandos House
5 & 6 Steadys Lane
Stanton Harcourt
Oxford OX29 5RL
UK
Tel: +44 (0) 1865 884447 Fax: +44 (0) 1865 884448
Email: info@chandospublishing.com
www.chandospublishing.com

First published in Great Britain in 2007

ISBN:
978 1 84334 349 3 (paperback)
978 1 84334 350 9 (hardback)
1 84334 349 5 (paperback)
1 84334 350 9 (hardback)

© Ravonne A. Green, 2007

British Library Cataloguing-in-Publication Data.
A catalogue record for this book is available from the British Library.

Typeset by Avocet Typeset, Chilton, Aylesbury, Bucks.
Printed in the UK and USA.

Contents

Acknowledgements   *vii*

Introduction   *ix*

About the authors   *xi*

PART 1 THE CASE STUDY AS RESEARCH TOOL

1   Why use the case study method?   3
     Ravonne A. Green

2   Case study basics   23
     Ravonne A. Green

3   Utilizing the case study approach for program evaluation   65
     Ravonne A. Green

PART 2 VALDOSTA STATE UNIVERSITY STUDENT CASE STUDIES

4   Special funding: use it or loose it   75
     Wendell C. Stone

5   Employee training   85
     Christopher Sharpe

6   Censorship issues   97
     Sammy Dees

7   Hiring decisions   107
     Nicol Lewis

8   To terminate or not to terminate, that is the question   113
     Matthew Sunrich

9   Privacy issues   123
     Haley Mims and Leah Dasher

10   A question of service: a case study of a bookmobile
     incident   127
     Tara McCann

11   Here's the new library, where are the staff?   143
     Maradith H. Sheffield

12   Can you teach an old dog new tricks?   147
     Kenneth N. McCullers

13   Conclusion   153
     Ravonne A. Green

Index   *159*

Acknowledgements

The case study method has always been a favorite teaching tool of mine for library management and leadership courses. One of the reasons that I have consistently used the case study method is because I have been convinced of its effectiveness. It is common for me to run into students some time after they have completed one of my courses and for them to mention a case study that they wrote in one of my classes or a case study that a classmate wrote.

This summer, in my library management class, I allowed more time to explore case studies more deeply. We wrote case studies, analyzed case studies, and explored alternative solutions. There is no correct way to manage a case study. There is no correct form for a case study. There is no correct solution to any problem.

These students worked hard and I encouraged them to publish their case studies at the end of the course. I gratefully acknowledge their efforts and support.

Introduction

Charles and Mertler (2002) identify three purposes of case study research: to provide vivid descriptions of an individual or phenomenon; to provide explanations; to provide evaluation data. Case study research can identify program strengths and weaknesses and may lead to modifications and improvements.

Case study research analysis involves developing and utilizing skills in evaluating the proposal, bounding the case study and analyzing the context, planning questions and criteria, identifying design and data collection methods, establishing and maintaining appropriate political, ethical and interpersonal relationships, collecting, analyzing and interpreting quantitative and qualitative data, reporting the case study, and evaluating the case study. This text deals with all of these issues.

Part 1 discusses the case study as a research tool. The first two chapters provide theoretical background for conducting a case study. The third chapter gives a model case study that outlines the elements and processes of a case study. The succeeding chapters in Part 2 include case studies written by library management students at Valdosta State University. The chapters include discussion questions, analyses, and alternative scenarios to provoke further thought and discussion.

Reference

Charles, C. and Mertler, C. (2002) *Introduction to Educational Research*. Boston: Allyn & Bacon.

About the authors

Ravonne A. Green is an Assistant Professor at Valdosta State University where she teaches management courses in the MLIS program. She received her PhD from Virginia Polytechnic Institute & State University and her MLIS from George Peabody College of Vanderbilt University. Dr Green had previous experience as a library director prior to assuming her current position at Valdosta State University.

All the MLIS management student contributors below have library experience and have been guided through the case study process in the MLIS 7200 management course.

Leah Dasher, Librarian, Southeastern Technical College, completed her Bachelor of Science degree in Business Administration at Brewton-Parker College and has a Master's degree in Management Information Systems from Strayer University. Leah is an MLIS student at Valdosta State University.

Sammy Dees, Admissions Counselor, Valdosta State University, is an MLIS student at Valdosta State University.

Alberta Ruth Hayden, Technical Services Librarian, Smyrna Public Library, Smyrna, Georgia, is an MLIS student at Valdosta State University.

Julia Huprich is currently employed as the Administrative Assistant at the Georgia College & State University Library and Instructional Technology Center. She hopes to graduate from Valdosta State University with her MLIS in May 2007.

Nicol Lewis, Helpdesk Manager, Georgia Public Library Service, is an MLIS student at Valdosta State University wishing to specialize in merging current technologies with traditional library practices.

Tara McCann, freelance writer and MLIS student at Valdosta State University and Wayne State University, served as a Children's Coordinator at South Georgia Regional Library in Valdosta before moving to Michigan.

Kenneth N. McCullers, Senior Library Specialist, DeKalb County Public Library and MLIS student at Valdosta State University, works in the Reference Department of the Decatur Library.

Haley Mims is a Valdosta State University MLIS student from Leesburg, Georgia.

Tonda Morris, Elementary Division Librarian, Whitefield Academy in the Metro Atlanta area has previous experience as a youth services librarian at the Smyrna Public Library and has worked in academic libraries. Tonda is also an MLIS student at Valdosta State University.

Christopher Sharpe, Circulation and Microform Library Paraprofessional I at Kennesaw State University, is also an MLIS student at Valdosta State University.

Maradith H. Sheffield, Information Technology Program

Chair/Librarian, Georgia Aviation Technical College, is an MLIS student at Valdosta State University.

Wendell C. Stone, Instructor, Mass Communications and Theatre Arts, University of West Georgia, Valdosta State University is an MLIS student.

Matthew Sunrich, Library Assistant at West Central Technical College in Waco, GA, is an MLIS student at Valdosta State University.

The authors may be contacted via the publishers.

Part 1

The case study as research tool

Why use the case study method?

Ravonne A. Green

Just-in-time (JIT) management has become a buzzword in management circles in recent years. When you go to have the oil changed in your car, the mechanic will call the auto parts store to order your oil filter. The courier will arrive a few minutes later with your oil filter. While you are having your oil changed, someone will come to bring a new bottle of spring water and place it on the dispenser. Another person will come and check the coffee pot and replace the coffee supply. Someone else will come and clean the restrooms and replenish the paper products. Someone will come and remove the mat at the front door and replace it with a clean one. Someone else will come and replenish the snack machine. Another person will come and replace the toner cartridges in the copier and printer and replenish the paper supplies. JIT management involves ordering parts, services, and, in some cases, personnel as needed.

JIT management ensures that a business does not have excessive inventory at the end of the year or pay for downtime when personnel are not needed. Part-time personnel are available on an as-needed basis to perform menial jobs. Clerical tasks may be performed from home or from a central office in order to cut down on human resources costs. Special projects may be parceled out to independent contractors who specialize in one certain task or the manufacture of certain goods. Research and development may occur in a foreign country or in your neighbor's basement.

JIT management has filtered into library management. Many technical service operations are completed at a central library or by a book jobber. We contract for online reference services, assessments, cafe, printer and copier supplies and services, and any number of other services and products. Instead of receiving truck loads of periodicals each month, we depend on electronic database aggregators to supply many titles online.

A new focus on problem-centered or case-based learning arose out of the JIT management movement. Case studies have been popular in the medical and legal profession for years. These studies tended to have a clinical, scientific outlook. They tended to focus on the individual and concentrated on fixing the problem for the individual. Business case studies focused on the organization and were primarily concerned with productivity. Many libraries are following the business model.

Case studies are research-informed stories that fuse some facet of theory with an aspect of practice (Mullen, 2006). Mullen (2006) further defines a case study as 'a selected problem that is studied by framing an inquiry, planning a course of action, searching for clues, generating tentative solutions, and keeping possibilities open.' Case studies involve well-developed characters, instill deep learning, and provide opportunities for testing theory and practice.

Barrows (1985) used the case study method in medical school. He divided students into small groups and assigned each student a problem patient. The task of the student group was to diagnose the patient applying previously learned medical knowledge and to prescribe a treatment. The students were provided with a mentor who listened to the group form hypotheses, generated questions regarding the diagnosis and treatment, and finally prescribed a treatment. The mentor provided guidance throughout the process. Albanese and Mitchell (1993) found that medical students using this approach retained their knowledge much longer than students in traditional classes. If you have ever watched *House, MD* on the television you have seen this general approach.

The case study method in educational and library settings shares elements of earlier models that have been used in medicine and business. However, the approach is much more constructivist. Using this approach, educators seek to provide grounding for problem-based learning first in the literature. The student then uses this knowledge to resolve professional problems.

Case studies are especially useful when examining controversial points of view and new theories, and provide a basis for future organizational problem-solving.

Duffy and Cunningham (1996) identify five strategies for problem-based learning.

1. *The problem as a guide.* Reading assignments are provided along with the case.

2. *The problem as an integrator or test.* The problem is presented after the readings, perhaps as an exam question. The case or problem gives the student the opportunity to apply knowledge from the readings. This process is similar to end-of-chapter review questions.

3. *The problem as an example.* The problem is integrated into the reading and is used to illustrate some principle, concept, or procedure.

4. *The problem as a vehicle for process.* The problem is presented as a means for developing critical thinking or problem-solving skills.

5. *The problem as a stimulus for authentic activity.* The focus of this strategy is much the same as the medical model. The student has an authentic opportunity to review an actual problem and to apply knowledge in the process of solving that problem.

Learning within an authentic context helps to prepare the student for real-life dilemmas. The instructor relinquishes the role of sage on the stage and instead gives guidance and support for self-directed learning in a collaborative environment and provides content knowledge as needed.

Allowing students to write their own case studies helps them to focus on real problems. Real problems tend to engage the learner and increased familiarity with the problem helps to alleviate questions and ambiguities. The focus is clearly on problem-solving and not on answering trivial questions.

The role of the facilitator is to provide additional information and to focus the student's attention on the critical issues involved with problem-solving. The facilitator may ask clarifying questions and make comments to encourage the student to go a little further in his/her analysis. No two managers will resolve a problem in the same manner. There is no specific form or method for case study research.

Case stories

It is perhaps important to differentiate between case studies and case stories. Case stories are another medium for delivering problem-based learning. There are many similarities in terms of scope and intent between case studies and case stories. In some cases, it is difficult to differentiate between the two methods.

A case study may be written by someone who is involved with the incident or problem. However, there are generally other people involved in assessing the case or problem. Even though the author of a case study may be involved in the case as an administrator or supervisor, typically the author will seek to corroborate his/her story with institutional documents and records and will have others involved in documenting and observing the case. The case study may be written for instructional purposes; however, it is sometimes written just to resolve one problem. The author of the case study seeks to maintain objectivity by documenting findings with professional literature and other resources both human and material.

A case story is written by an individual and is clearly told from the author's perspective. We often refer to case stories as 'war stories' in the classroom. Many professors contribute valuable stories from their experience that serve as learning models. The Harvard Leadership Institute and several similar programs utilize the case story method to illustrate best practice in our profession. The case story method often blends aspects of the case study method with the art of storytelling. Stories told by or about significant figures are particularly effective.

Maslin-Ostrowski and Ackerman (2006) recommend five steps for effectively sharing a case story.

1. Participants are given a seven-minute writing exercise intended to ease them into writing about leadership and practice from a personal perspective. They are divided into small groups where they discuss case story guidelines (see step 3).

2. After reviewing an example, participants are guided to write a one-page narrative about a professional dilemma that matters to them.

3. Participants take turns telling, listening to, and discussing case stories. After each participant has told his/her story there is one minute of silence, after which participants may ask only clarifying questions. Listeners may not give advice or share personal examples. The goal is not to solve the problem for the storyteller, but to assist him or her in understanding what happened and to find his or her own meaning in the difficult experience.

4. Small groups merge and begin to reflect on the process.

5. The whole group reflects and reports on learning, and the facilitator reinforces the importance of understanding ourselves in order to improve professional practice.

Case stories help participants to develop the competence and confidence to solve problems. Case stories also serve an instructional purpose, at least for the author, in providing an opportunity to process events and to reflect on the lessons learned from this incident. The *Journal of Cases in Educational Leadership* (*JCEL*) provides a meaningful forum for educators and administrators who wish to share research-based experiences. Their website is *http://www.ucea .org/cases*.

Case stories focus on developing the individual. The stories may be helpful to others and often are but they are primarily introspective. There is no evidence base for case stories. Case studies focus on developing interpersonal skills while collecting and analyzing data and building arguments based on evidence (Mullen, 2006).

The purposes of case studies

The first case that you will read in this book is clearly a case study. Wendell C. Stone describes a new library director's plight involving grant funding for a new library addition. This case study takes the reader through the decision-making and planning process for accepting and expending the grant funds.

Charles and Mertler (2002) identify three purposes of case study research. The first is to provide vivid descriptions of an individual or phenomenon. For example, a library researcher may wish to provide outcomes data to demonstrate the effectiveness of an information literacy program. The researcher might conduct in-depth interviews with six seniors that took Information Competency 101 at the beginning of their freshman year and have attended a series of Information Competency courses each year for the last four years. The researcher may select six seniors that are enrolled in the same major that did not take the information competency courses and compare the results among students within this major. The researcher may select seniors from six different majors and compare results across the curriculum. The researcher may decide to have two separate groups and to compare the results from both groups.

A second purpose for case study research is to provide explanations. Often quantitative research raises 'why' questions. It is not sufficient to know that the circulation count has been down. Case study research seeks to identify behavioral and procedural patterns. A case study researcher might notice that the circulation count is down 85 percent in the English literature section, accounting for the majority of the overall decrease in circulation. S/he decides to do a case study of this phenomenon and begins to set up interviews with a sample group of faculty and students that have taught or have been enrolled in English literature courses this year. This case study should point out relational patterns. Relational patterns indicate that two or more events or traits appear to be related. For example, Mr Smith who has taught English literature for the past twenty years at ABC University required his students to each check out ten books the second week of class for their term papers. Mr Smith retired last spring and his successor did not require term papers. Therefore the fact that the new English literature professor does not require term papers is probably related to the decrease in the English literature circulation count.

Explanations sometimes point out causal patterns. We typically think of causal patterns as negative influences. The researcher definitely wants to identify causal factors and report these. For example, if a shifting project is occurring and the English literature section has been moved to another floor and there are no directional signs, patrons may be extremely frustrated if they have come to the library to check out English literature books and cannot find them.

The third purpose of case study research is to provide evaluation data. Case study research is useful for evaluating programs, individuals, and settings. Case study research can identify program strengths and weaknesses and may lead to modifications and improvements. A strengths, weaknesses, opportunities, and threats (SWOT) analysis may identify general areas of strength and weakness. A case study researcher can then analyze these areas more thoroughly by interviewing individuals or conducting an in-depth program evaluation.

Russ-Eft and Preskill (2001) suggest five uses for case studies within the context of teaching and learning that could well be applied to the library setting:

- how employees are using what they learned from a training event;
- why employee performance is at a certain level;
- the ways in which individuals learn from technology-based instruction;
- how the organization supports or inhibits individual, team, and organizational learning and change; and
- what effect reorganization has had on a certain group of employees.

The case study approach is an excellent qualitative research method where factors and relationships may be directly observed. Fidel (1984) suggests that case studies are also appropriate when a large variety of factors and relationships are being studied and when there are no criteria for ranking factors and relationships. Case study researchers attempt to gather in-depth material related to an individual or to a program or event. Powell and Connaway (2004) suggest a case study for an investigation of staff burnout in a reference department. The case study data would be further corroborated with questionnaires, interviews, observation, and document analysis. Case studies are particularly effective for longitudinal studies and for studies having a lot of complex issues.

Robert Stake (1978) encouraged evaluators to focus on a program within its immediate context. Stake argued that grounding a study within a bounded case helped to construct a more comprehensive understanding of the case. Creswell (1998) identifies this bounded system as an individual, program, event, or activity that is being studied. Creswell (1998) further defines *multi-site study* as several programs being studied and *within-site study* as a single program. Van Dalen (1966) describes cases studies as an endeavor to trace interrelationships between facts that will provide a deeper phenomenal insight.

Russ-Eft and Preskill (2001) list the following advantages of the case study design:

- provides descriptive data;

- does not require manipulation or control of individuals or setting;

- reports include verbatim quotes of interviewees;

- leads to a greater understanding about the context of the evaluation;

- leads to greater understanding about practice;

- tends to gather data using multiple methods (triangulation);

- provides data that are rich with examples and stories;

- captures what is important to participants;

- portrays the multiplicity of causes associated with outcomes;

- embraces the diversity of participants' perspectives and experiences;

- Allows the evaluator to collect information on outcomes not known or anticipated prior to the learning and performance initiative.

Russ-Eft and Preskill (2001: 174) also identify the following disadvantages to the case study design:

- results do not lead to scientific generalizability;

- evaluator bias may interfere with validity of findings;

- may take too long to conduct;

- may produce more data than can be analyzed in a timely or cost-effective way.

Types of case study

Eisner (1991) points out that even though case study researchers center their attention on one individual or program, they often include themes representing concrete universals and morals that may be generalized to similar situations. These naturalistic generalizations may either be *particularistic, instrumental,* or *collective case studies.*

Particularistic case studies focus on a particular individual or problem. Particularistic cases are sometimes referred to as *intrinsic case studies* (Stake, 1995). The researcher has an interest in the case. Particularistic case studies deal with understanding or interpreting an individual's behavior or attitude. Since particularistic case studies focus on an individual, the researcher will include extensive descriptions of the individual who is the focus of the case study. Particularistic case studies are thick with character analysis. Character analysis does not just involve telling a story about an individual but means getting to the root of what has caused this person to react in a certain manner. The researcher looks for consistencies and inconsistencies. The researcher might, for example, notice that the individual that is being studied reacts one way to one individual and in another manner toward someone else in a similar circumstance. If this individual is a library director, the library director may appear to be extremely accommodating toward administrators but act in a condescending manner toward subordinates. A circulation librarian may permit an administrator to check out a stack of books without producing a library card even though a sign by the circulation desk states that all patrons must have a library card in order to check out books. This same librarian may deny a college freshman the privilege to check out books when s/he cannot produce a library card. The focus throughout the case study is clearly on the individual and the fact that the individual is perceived as being the problem. The researcher attempts to give credence to the individual as the seat of the problem by presenting as many conflict situations as possible where the individual reacts in a negative fashion.

Particularistic studies generally occur over time in order to give the researcher the opportunity to adequately and accurately observe an individual's behavior. Particularistic case studies are typically just useful in dealing with one person; however, they can sometimes be generalized to similar character types. We have all had the experience of reading a case study that was written about a library employee in a far away place and exclaiming, 'I know this person!' In fact, we generally do not know this particular person but someone that has character traits that are amazingly similar.

Particularistic studies typically do not deal with just one isolated incident. Sometimes employees can point back to one incident that was the catalyst for a negative chain of events. However, this one incident typically is indicative of this person's general behavior and attitudes. An interviewee might make a comment like, 'That was when he showed his true colors!' Such comments let the case study researcher know that the incident that the interviewee has just reported was the beginning of the awareness of the problem with this individual. Denzin (1989) refers to such a moment as 'the major epiphany.'

There are also 'cumulative epiphanies' when an individual overreacts to a situation based on pent up stresses (Denzin, 1989). An extreme example of a cumulative epiphany would be if someone went on a wild shooting spree injuring several library employees. Lesser extreme examples have occurred in most libraries at some point. For example, Sue may report to her supervisor that 'all she did was say "good morning" to Jack and he bit my head off.' As a researcher, you might mention this incident to Jack. Jack might inform you that he was very angry with Sue on that morning because she was scheduled to help him with two bibliographic instruction sessions at 8:00 a.m. and 9:00 a.m. She had not shown up for either one of them and he had been left to manage the reference desk alone and had not had a break all morning. Sue had done this to him repeatedly over the last year. He had reported her behavior to his supervisor and she had done nothing. She seemed always to defend Sue. When Sue finally arrived at 10:45 a.m., Jack admits that he lost his temper.

Particularistic case studies may be instructive but their main purpose is for documentation. The comments that are included in the case study may also be used in an instructive manner with the individual that is involved in an attempt to resolve issues or problems. The comments may be used in a memo or letter to the individual that suggests or requires corrective action.

Single program case studies begin with individual case studies, then the cross-case analysis of the individual cases. Patton (1990) identifies three layers of case studies: individual participant case studies at project sites combined to make up project site case studies; project site case studies combined to make up state case studies; and state programs combined to make up a national program case study. Van Dalen (1966) discusses case studies as a vehicle for probing in depth to examine the total life cycle of a social unit or to focus on a specific phase.

Instrumental case studies are used to solve a research question or a general management problem. Instrumental case studies can be generalized to more than one setting. Instrumental case studies may be used to resolve library issues involving circulation or reference statistics, budget issues, construction dilemmas, marketing challenges, or to provide training on legal, disability, or multicultural awareness issues.

Instrumental case studies may be based on one issue and are useful for resolving similar issues. Instrumental case studies can be used as a form of brainstorming. A library director or department chair may present a brief case study describing a scenario that involves a current library problem or issue and ask all of the participants to write or discuss a solution. An administrator may present a case study in response to a research question or to facilitate the understanding of a problem.

Instrumental case studies typically start with a topical or research question. The topical question is followed by a foreshadowed problem, the foreshadowed problem is thoroughly investigated by the researcher, and the researcher makes logical assertions based on his/her initial questions, investigations of the issue or problem within a specific environment, and supportive documentation. Stake (1995) insists that the absolutely essential elements of a case study are the definition of the case including the context, the list of research questions, the identification of research assistants or participants, the data sources, the allocation of time, expenses, and the intended reporting strategies and timelines. Cresswell (1998) includes analysis techniques such as holistic analysis, embedded analysis, and within-case and cross-case analysis.

A third type of case study is the *collective case study*. A collective case study involves reviewing a group of similar cases in order to determine similar trends, issues, or problems. Data are collected and synthesized in order to identify commonalities.

Fitzpatrick et al. (2004) point out that a case study does not have a clearly delineated method. Lincoln and Guba

(1985) focus on the case study as a means for reporting observation results. Stake (1978) focused on what is to be accomplished. Whatever the focus, the case study is much more informal and subjective than quantitative designs. Everything that is reported is intended to provide a complex, holistic view of the case. The case study does not always just involve observations. The case analysis may include quantitative data, institutional data and records, surveys, interviews, and anything that is relevant to the case. We will review a hypothetical collective case study in Chapter 3 which employs a mixed-methods approach.

Chapter glossary

Case definition or context   The environmental factors such as facility details, departmental flow charts, budgets, policies, special circumstances, and assessment data all help to provide information about the context of the case and the case boundaries.

Case study   A research strategy in which varied types of evidence may be collected ranging from archival records to first-hand and second-hand accounts of thoughts and actions by various methods such as interviews, quantitative data, and focus group reports (Case, 2002).

Collective case studies   These involve reviewing a group of similar cases in order to determine similar trends, issues, or problems. Data are collected and synthesized in order to identify commonalities.

Cross-case analysis   This involves reviewing at least two cases in a holistic manner and comparing the results.

Data sources   These include any information that may be useful to the researcher in documenting and assessing the case.

Embedded analysis   An analysis of a specific aspect of a case.

Holistic analysis   The case study researcher will want to include data from a number of sources in order to gain a clear understanding of the case. Getting a clear picture of an employee's absence record might include interviewing a supervisor and several colleagues, and reviewing sick leave and annual leave forms, medical reports, and work flow statistics.

Instrumental case studies   These are used to solve a research question or a general management problem. Instrumental case studies can be generalized to more than one setting.

Participants   The primary stakeholders should be identified in the early stages of the case study. The participants will include the individuals or the program that is being studied as well as the individuals that will be using the study.

Particularistic case studies   These focus on a particular individual or problem. Particularistic cases are also referred to as *intrinsic case studies*. Particularistic case studies deal with understanding or interpreting an individual's behavior or attitudes.

Reporting strategies   The thorough case study researcher will want to provide regular feedback for the stakeholders. Feedback may be in the form of e-mails, telephone conversations, formal meetings, and reports. There should be opportunities for discussion with the stakeholders and the stakeholder's comments and suggestions should be a part of the reporting process and the final report.

Reporting timelines   The researcher and the stakeholders should form and agree upon a tentative timeline in the initial stages of the study.

Research questions   The case should address a set of

questions that the stakeholders wish to answer. These may involve questions about program assessment and effectiveness or individual performance.

Within-case analysis This involves reviewing the same case within different contexts. For example, Mary might do an excellent job when she works at the reference desk but her statistics in technical services are abysmal. The case study researcher would want to get to the root of what the problem is when Mary works in technical services. She may have not had adequate training in technical services, she may have a personality conflict with someone in that department, or she may have some disability that affects her work in technical services.

Focus questions

1. Keeping in mind the three purposes of case study research, describe an instance when it might be appropriate to use this method at your library.

2. What are the uses for case studies other than those identified by Russ-Eft and Preskill (2001)?

Application exercises

1. Select a topic for case study research.

2. Describe the particular advantages in using the case study method for your research project.

3. Describe the disadvantages in using the case study method for your project.

4. After reviewing the three types of case studies, identify your case study type.

References and further reading

Albanese, M. and Mitchell, S. (1993) 'Problem-based learning: a review of the literature on its outcomes and implementation issues,' *Academic* Medicine, 68: 52–81.

Barrows, H. (1985) *How to Design a Problem-based Curriculum for the Preclinical Years.* New York: Springer.

Case, D. (2002) *Looking for Information: A Survey of Research on Information Seeking, Needs, and Behavior.* San Diego, CA: Academic Press.

Charles, C. and Mertler, C. (2002) *Introduction to Educational Research.* Boston: Allyn & Bacon.

Creswell, J. (1998) *Qualitative Inquiry and Research Design: Choosing Among Five Traditions.* Thousand Oaks, CA: Sage.

Denzin, N. (1989). *Interpretive Biography,* Qualitative Research Methods 17. Thousand Oaks, CA : Sage.

Denzin, N. and Lincoln, Y. (1998) *Collecting and Interpreting Qualitative Materials.* Thousand Oaks, CA: Sage.

Duffy, T. and Cunningham, D. (1996) 'Constructivism: implications for the design and delivery of instruction,' in D. Jonassen (ed.), *Handbook of Research for Educational Communications and Technology.* New York: Macmillan.

Eisner, E.W. (1991) *The Enlightened Eye: Qualitative Inquiry and the Enhancement of Educational Practice.* New York: Macmillan.

Fidel, R. (1984) 'The case study method: a case study,' *Library and Information Science Research,* 6: 274.

Fitzpatrick, J., Sanders, J., and Worthen, B. (2004) *Program Evaluation: Alternative Approaches and Practical Guidelines,* 3rd edn. Boston: Allyn & Bacon.

Lincoln, Y. and Guba, E. (1985) *Naturalistic Inquiry.* Thousand Oaks, CA: Sage.

Maslin-Ostrowski, P. and Ackerman, R. (2004) *Adult Learning Methods: A Guide for Effective Instruction*, 3rd edn. MFL: Krieger.

Mullen, C. (2006) 'Case studies,' in F. English (ed.), *Encyclopedia of Educational Leadership and Administration*, Vol. 1. Thousand Oaks, CA: Sage.

Patton, M. (1990) *Qualitative Evaluation and Research Methods*, 2nd edn. Newbury Park, CA: Sage.

Patton, M. (2002) *Qualitative Research and Evaluation Methods.* Thousand Oaks, CA: Sage.

Powell, R. and Connaway, L. (2004) *Basic Research Methods for Librarians*, 4th edn, Library and Information Science Text Series. Westport, CT: Libraries Unlimited.

Russ-Eft, D. and Preskill, H. (2001) *Evaluation in Organizations.* Cambridge, MA: Perseus.

Stake, R. (1978) *The Case Study Method in Social Inquiry.* Thousand Oaks, CA: Sage.

Stake, R. (1995) *The Art of Case Study Research.* Thousand Oaks, CA: Sage.

Van Dalen, D. (1966) *Understanding Educational Research.* New York: McGraw-Hill.

Case study basics

Ravonne A. Green

Context of the case

The researcher should provide information about the physical setting as well as details about the social, historical, and economic influences that form the context of the case. The context provides a preliminary description of the setting and some preliminary information on how this context will be interpreted such as the analysis of themes and assertions. The context of the case helps to *bound* the case in terms of time, events, and processes.

Case expectations

One of the first questions that we ask when someone comes to visit our facility is, 'How long will you be staying?' Everyone involved in the case study should have a clear picture of the time that will be allotted for interviews, observations, and other evaluative processes. The researcher should clearly identify human resources and materials that will be needed in order to conduct the case study. The researcher's contract should clearly delineate all expenses.

Definition of the problem or description of the case

The researcher should define the problem or describe the case, providing the stakeholders with the preliminary investigative questions regarding the case. The researcher should be careful not to provide superfluous details but should provide all of the details that the reader might need to answer questions about why this person or this group may have reacted in a certain manner. If the fact that the library director is wearing a red tie is in some way connected with the observation at hand, the researcher should include that detail. However, if the red tie has no relevance to the rest of the narrative, it should be omitted. The case study researcher will make a lot of field notes initially that may or may not be included in the final report because they are not relevant.

An individual or particularistic case study may begin with a description of the person and a general statement concerning the problem behaviors that this person is presenting in his/her environment. Studies involving a program or activity may begin with a general statement about the perceived problem(s) within this program or activity. Instrumental case studies may begin with a general statement of the problem, issue, or training that is under consideration.

The problem definition and the initial descriptors provide background information to answer the *what* and *how* questions connected with the case. This background information gives the reader a sense of the problem and the environment. The problem definition and case description may establish focal points and boundaries about cases and sub-cases to be studied.

Sampling

Patton (1990) lists 15 strategies for selecting sampling types. The most common sampling involves selecting critical cases, extreme cases, typical cases, and varied cases. The logic and power of probability sampling depends on selecting a random and statistically representative sample that will justify generalizations to a larger population. However, the power and logic of purposeful sampling lies in selecting information-rich cases for in-depth study. For example, if the purpose of the case study is to determine the relevance of a new chemistry database for chemistry students, the researcher will want a purposeful sample that accurately represents this group. She may select ten chemistry PhD students for interviews. The following strategies are suggested by Patton (1990) for selecting purposeful samples for information-rich cases. Examples of library applications are provided for each strategy.

Extreme or deviant case sampling

These cases are either outstanding failures or successes. Down-and-Out Library in Poorville, USA was located in a bad section of town. Gang activity was rampant. Children never came to the library. Karen Jones moved to Poorville and accepted a job as the library director. Karen immediately decided that she was going to change her environment. She went to visit the local probation officer and asked him to set up interviews with some of the gang members in the neighborhood. After completing a series of interviews, Karen completed her case analysis and determined that she would start a literacy program for young teens. She had learned from her data the materials that would be most appropriate for this group and the incentives that would be most appealing to them, and had established a rapport with these individuals.

Intensity sampling

Intensity sampling is less extreme than deviant sampling. It is often used in heuristic research to describe phenomena or emotions. For example, a case study researcher might wish to do a study on feelings of isolation and loneliness among mid-level library managers. The researcher would then select a group of mid-level library managers and might either interview them individually or ask them to complete a survey about isolation and loneliness issues. The researcher might use both techniques with the same group in order to further validate the results using a mixed methodology. The researcher might cross-analyze the results and determine the prevalence of feelings of loneliness and isolation among mid-level managers and might perhaps suggest some strategies for overcoming these problems.

Maximum variation sampling

Maximum variation sampling is used particularly in impact studies to capture central themes and principal outcomes. Common patterns that emerge using this technique are of particular interest to the researcher. The value is in capturing the core experiences and the shared aspects or impacts of a program. For example, Bob might be evaluating a nationwide library program. Bob decides that he will contact library directors that are members of the Association of College and Research Libraries and visit 20 of these librarians and interview them about this program. These 20 librarians are all from different states so Bob will have adequate variation in sampling. Bob will not take these results and generalize the results to a national population but will instead look for information that identifies programmatic variation and significant common patterns within that variation.

Homogeneous samples

Homogeneous sampling is the opposite of maximum variation sampling. The point of homogeneous sampling is to describe a particular subgroup in detail. Focus groups are typically homogeneous groups that examine issues using open-ended questions in a group interview setting. A case study researcher, Jane, might conduct a focus group with a group of college seniors that have never used the library. Jane would use the data from this group interview to determine underlying causes for library apathy among this group and possible solutions for this problem.

Typical case sampling

Typical cases are usually selected by key informants, program staff, and knowledgeable participants. These individuals can identify what is 'typical.' Typical cases can be selected electronically using software to find averages and modal scores from survey data.

The purpose of reporting typical cases is to illustrate or define what is typical to someone who may not be familiar with a program. For example, the manufacturer of a new copier designed for large books that automatically turns the pages is interested in conducting a series of case studies with a group of 'typical' libraries across the United States. They ask Mr Don Charming to select 50 typical libraries. Mr

Charming reviews usage data and averages the results. Mr Charming compiles a list of 50 libraries from his current customer list that make an average number of copies per year. He contacts these libraries and requests permission to set up his new copiers at their universities. He agrees to allow these libraries to have a 30-day free trial of the copier in exchange for keeping an observation log in which they record problems and patron comments and doing an in-depth interview at the end of the 30 days. Mr Charming will use these data to identify problems with the copier and to record customer satisfaction comments.

Stratified purposeful sampling

Stratified purposeful sampling involves selecting layers or strata to examine variations. Stratified purposeful sampling may be considered a thicker version of maximum variation sampling. Instead of having one person from a certain category, you may interview five people from each category. The purpose of this technique is to identify commonalities among groups such as socioeconomic or political groups. These groups are typically too small to generalize the results to a larger population but they do identify common issues that may be useful for further testing.

Critical case sampling

Critical cases make a dramatic point. Typically a key informant provides observation data to indicate that if an event occurred in this setting, it could happen anywhere.

Diane McWhirley, a library director at Midville College, was astounded to hear that a reference librarian at South Central Bible College had recently shot her close friend, Tina

Walters, the library director, two other librarians, and several students before shooting himself. She had visited Tina on several occasions at South Central and had always remarked about the calm, serene setting. Tina's small staff all seemed like family. Diane could not imagine that such an awful tragedy could have occurred at South Central. Diane contacted the Vice-President for Academic Affairs at South Central and asked if she could interview the librarians. Diane wants to make sense of this situation because she is convinced that if such a tragedy could occur at South Central, it could happen anywhere. Diane will look for anything that might explain the bizarre behavior of the individual that committed this act. She will be concerned with potential solutions that the librarians might have for preventing this sort of tragedy on other campuses.

Critical cases are used to demonstrate potential effectiveness. For example, if a library with extremely limited funds has a highly effective program, a researcher might conclude that any library could deliver similar results based on the cost per student ratio.

Snowball or chain sampling

This process involves contacting key informants and asking to talk with experts on a given topic. The process starts with a question like, 'Who should I talk to about . . .' or 'Who knows a lot about . . .' The snowball gets bigger and bigger as one person mentions an expert and that expert in turn mentions someone else.

Tom wants to research the effectiveness of a new assistive technology in libraries. Tom contacts his friend Joe Lazzaro who wrote the book, *Adaptive Technologies for Learning and Work Environments*. Joe agrees to meet with Tom for an interview. Joe talks to Tom about his experiences with assistive technology and then suggests that Tom should meet his friend Norm Coombs at the Rochester Institute of Technology. Tom contacts Norm and Norm agrees to meet with Tom for an interview. Norm then suggests that Tom should meet with Jeromy Elkind at Kurzweil. Tom contacts Jeromy and he agrees to meet with him for an interview.

Tom continues to meet with another ten people who tell him about their experiences with using this new assistive technology based on their individual areas of expertise. They all identify certain areas of weakness in their expertise but recommend other experts that can fill in these gaps. Tom is able to gain a holistic picture of the effectiveness of this technology by interviewing all of these experts. The Peters and Waterman (1982) study *In Search of Excellence* began with snowball sampling. *The Change Masters* (1983) by Rosabeth Moss Kanter is another example of a study that utilized this technique.

Criterion sampling

Criterion sampling is typically used when a phenomenon cannot be explained for a given case or for one group or program.

Janice and Carl have taught an information skills class for the last five years. They have always been proud of their post-test scores because they have been significantly higher than the pre-test scores. This semester, Janice and Carl are puzzled by one entire set of scores. One entire class scored lower on the post-test scores than they had scored on the pre-test. They remember that this group was unusually attentive and appeared to be engaged in the learning process. They decide to interview twelve students from this class in order to get in-depth responses about the problems with these scores.

Theory-based or operational construct sampling

The researcher samples incidents, time periods, or people based on important theoretical constructs. These constructs or entities are usually legally or financially defined. An operational construct is a real-world example and the study of several examples that fit within this construct would be considered 'multiple operationalism.'

Catherine decides that she is going to study Americans with Disabilities Act (ADA) compliance issues in academic libraries in her state. She reviews Title III of the ADA and develops a compliance matrix. She then develops a questionnaire based on this matrix and posts it on the listserv for her state library organization. These steps will help Catherine to develop a theoretical construct. Catherine decides to visit all of the academic libraries that have responded to the questionnaire to conduct in-depth interviews with the library directors and other librarians that are involved with providing special services. She has made the leap to multiple operationalism. Catherine will use responses from the questionnaire, some research questions that she has developed, and some hunches from her observations to form her interview questions.

Catherine collects brochures, URLs, policy statements, product literature, surveys from patrons with special needs, and other documentation to corroborate her fieldnotes. Catherine establishes codes for recording her fieldnotes before she begins the interviews. She will transfer her coded data from her fieldnotes to the matrices that she developed at the beginning of the process. She will review her completed matrices and all of her data and will make appropriate judgements about ADA compliance issues at academic libraries in her state. Her data may then be disseminated to other libraries and used for benchmarking or comparison purposes.

Confirming and disconfirming cases

The act of finding and reporting data from confirming as well as disconfirming cases involves extreme rigor on the part of the researcher. Confirming cases fit already established categories or emerging patterns. These cases further confirm findings and add richness and depth. Disconfirming cases are the outliers. Disconfirming cases are the exceptions to the rule. While disconfirming cases may not serve to validate the case, they do serve to confirm the credibility of the researcher and often provide a source for further research and investigation.

Steve Milligan has just returned from a conference where he attended a session on disability awareness training. He was particularly interested in one training presentation because it involved a library similar in size and scope to his library. The library director cited impact results that indicated that this program had been highly successful at her library. Steve talked with her after the session and she agreed to send him all of her training materials and to come to his library to help with a training session. As Steve talked with her, she proudly told him about students with learning disabilities who had become engaged in library research.

The reference librarians had all attended a course on specific learning disabilities. Now that the reference librarians knew how to address these students' specific disabilities, they were capable of identifying their specific needs and providing library resources and instructional methods that were appropriate for the students' needs. The library director told stories about students with print disabilities that were using the Kurzweil software and other tools to accomplish their research and were making significant academic gains. She mentioned that they had moved all of the assistive technology out into the middle of the library so that it would be easily accessible for patrons and library staff could easily see when someone needed help with the equipment. Then she said:

> Perhaps I shouldn't mention that we have had one very disappointing dilemma. After we moved all of the assistive technology out into the middle of the library we noticed that one girl that had come to the library regularly to use the Kurzweil quit coming. One of our reference librarians saw her on campus and she said that she felt totally humiliated to sit where everyone could see her reading large print on a screen out in the middle of the library. Another young man with a hearing problem reported that he would no longer use the TTY machine because it was in the middle of the library.

Steve has just been told about two disconfirming cases. He asks the library director if she could give him contact information for these individuals so that he can get some further information from them about how to develop a more inclusive and yet private environment for patrons with disabilities at his library.

Opportunistic sampling

While case study research should be structured to some extent it is good to remain open to new opportunities. You will meet individuals in the course of your interviews or observations that you had not planned to interview but who may have significant data or experiences to add to the study.

You may determine later that it is not appropriate to include these impromptu interviews. It is better to take the risk and decide that you will not need or cannot use the information later than to neglect mining some gem that may shed an important light on the case.

Carol is interviewing technical services librarians regarding a new systems project that they have initiated. The librarians invite her to the library café for coffee and the director of campus systems support joins them. He immediately begins to talk about the new Oracle-based system and some of the challenges that he faces in trying to migrate current data and to interface this system with the current network. Carol had not planned to interview him but she decides that perhaps he might fill in some gaps regarding the technology that the librarians have not answered.

Purposeful random sampling

Random sampling may be used in qualitative research as well as quantitative. Impact studies or war stories are sometimes the most effective technique for demonstrating effectiveness. However, this technique can be made more credible using randomized sampling. War stories demonstrate effectiveness after the fact. Purposeful random sampling seeks to select potential participants randomly based on a set of pre-determined criteria. Using this technique, the researcher establishes a set list of criteria for participants and has participants complete a questionnaire to determine if they are an appropriate fit for the study.

Shamika is trying a new women's studies database in the reference department for 30 days. She talked with the women's studies professor and asked her to agree to bring her class to the library for training the first week that the database was available. Shamika has noticed that this professor has told several of her friends about the database and they have come in to use it. Also, word seems to have circulated among the students about the new database.

Shamika has been asked to do a training session for an English class so that they can use the database for a research paper on women authors. Shamika knows that this database is expensive and that she will need to make a powerful statement to her director in order to persuade her to provide the funding for this new database. Shamika develops a questionnaire with open-ended questions designed to inform her of the types of research that individuals have conducted who were using the database as well as their perceptions of the database. She asks a couple of probing questions because she wants something more than 'This is awesome!' Shamika distributes her questionnaires to the two professors who have brought their classes to the library for training and asks them to distribute them in class. Students will be asked to include their names and contact information if they are willing to be approached for further information.

Shamika sets up a list of criteria that she will be looking for as she reviews the questionnaires. She develops a matrix where she will code her data and enter the results. When the questionnaires are returned to Shamika, she enters the results in the matrix and notes patterns and similarities. She contacts the students and professors that she has identified as providing the most powerful information and asks to meet with them individually for a follow-up interview. Shamika asks more in-depth questions during her in-depth interviews and will present a final report to the director based on her most powerful impact statements.

Shamika initially randomized her sample by distributing

the questionnaires to both classes. She concluded with a purposeful random sample by exploring the results of her questionnaire and determining the individuals who would be the best fit for her data.

Sampling politically important cases

The case study researcher must be aware of and sensitive to political influences that are involved in a case study. During an election year, political acumen is extremely important. Todd has met Representative Gates once at a fundraiser. He chatted with Gates briefly about adult literacy, mentioning that his library was awarded an adult literacy grant and that they have just completed the funding cycle. A few months later Todd learns that Gates is running for senator. Todd is aware that a branch library located in Representative Gates's district has just completed an adult literacy program that they perceived as being highly effective. Todd immediately contacts the branch manager and asks her to complete a series of interviews and to conduct a cross-analysis and synthesize the results to document the effectiveness of this program. Todd will collect this data and write a letter to Representative Gates including specific high-impact statements from the case study reports and requesting funding for another funding cycle.

Convenience sampling

Convenience sampling is by far the most familiar and the most often used sampling strategy. These cases are easily accessible and inexpensive. The main problem with convenience sampling is that there are typically no controls and they have little reliability. Convenience sampling is neither purposeful nor strategic. Additionally, there may be significant privacy issues involved with convenience sampling. While the researcher should engage the reader, case studies are not just creative stories.

Sarah has been assigned a case study to write for her library management class. Sarah immediately thinks about her library director, Elmer Hamilton. Elmer is the strangest creature on the face of the earth and Sarah decides that the entire class and even the professor will be well entertained with her tales about Elmer. She does not think about a strategy for her case study. She does not need any documents. Elmer stories will be sufficient by themselves without any other documentation. She writes her tales using expressive adjectives. She describes Elmer's unsavoury friends from the city hall that come to visit every day. She describes Elmer's lack of fashion skills including the totally unfashionable tie that he wears every day that has an accumulation of every spaghetti dinner that he has ever eaten at the local Moose Lodge.

Sarah is astounded when she receives an e-mail from her professor reminding her of her earlier admonition against using convenience sampling. The professor's note further chastises her for ignoring all the canons of scientific research. Sarah has not included the context for her case study, a definition of the problem other than her perception that Mr Hamilton is weird. There are no research questions, no hypotheses, no evidence of a conceptual framework, no investigation, no appropriate assertions, no triangulation, and her data cannot be generalized in any way.

Sampling choices for multiple case studies should be representative of the primary case. Purposeful sampling indicates an understanding of the problem that is being studied as well as laying the groundwork for generalizability. The case study researcher will typically select cases that offer as many perspectives as possible on the problem, process, program, or activity. If the focus is on an individual or an individual program as an exemplary case, the researcher will need to establish criteria for identifying the case. There may be times when a researcher cannot gain access to the individual or program that is most desirable and must settle for a similar case that is accessible.

Instrumentation

Instrumentation deals with designing an effective instrument that adheres to the constructs of validity and reliability, and minimizes researcher bias within a descriptive-contextual setting.

Research questions and conceptual organizers

Some case study researchers, particularly for instrumental or instructive case studies, like to provide research questions to guide the process and to engage the reader. Parlett and Hamilton (1976) call this technique 'progressive focusing.' Stake (1995) states that 'good research questions are especially important for case studies because case and context are infinitely complex and the phenomena are fluid and elusive.' Good research questions help to ground the researcher's observations in areas that are most relevant. Some case study researchers produce a list of issues or problem statements to guide the reader. Information questions may be included to suggest the need for additional information. For example, the researcher may report an incident and ask the question, 'What is the library's policy on this issue?' These questions may be included in the preliminary report and replaced with more complete information in the final report. Evaluative questions may be included to determine the value of certain programs. For example, a librarian may mention the library's information literacy program. The researcher might insert the question: 'How effective is the information literacy program?' In the final report, the researcher might insert survey data or some form of outcomes assessment that measures the effectiveness of the information literacy program. Since instrumental case studies deal with a specific problem or issue, it behooves the case study researcher to substantiate his/her findings with specific data.

Patton (1990) cites a number of government studies (Chew, 1989; Tilney and Riordan, 1988; Johnston et al., 1987; Binnendijk, 1986; Warren, 1984; Rogers and Wallerstein, 1985; Bremer, 1985; Wasserman and Davenport, 1983; Steinberg, 1983). These are all classic impact studies demonstrating the synthesis of direct fieldwork, project documents, interviews, and observations to draw policy-relevant conclusions from individual project case studies.

Research questions do not have to be hypothesis statements for case studies. They may serve as hypotheses but their main purpose is to conceptualize the framework for the study.

Peshkin (1985) recommends re-titling the case study several times in the process of writing it in order to gain different perspectives. The list of issues and research questions will change each time the title changes. This technique helps the researcher to maintain a non-biased perspective and to construct an objective framework for the reader.

Foreshadowing

Foreshadowing involves a global examination of the problem. The case study researcher might mention recent journal articles or books about the topical problem, institutional research, or a similar library problem at another university or in another community. For example, a case study that is investigating a library marketing plan might mention the increasing need for library marketing and recent books and articles on the subject. This section should focus on libraries that are as similar as possible to the one that is being investigated. While this section is not an extensive literature review, it should provide a broad coverage of current materials and resources on the topic under investigation.

Investigating

According to Stake (1995) the aim of a case study researcher in presenting a problem is to provide the reader or researcher with an understanding of the problem. The case study researcher must be an astute observer of human behavior and have an acumen for problem-solving. Case studies are not just entertaining stories. The narrative observation is intended to provide information to substantiate a claim or problem, to instruct, inform, or motivate the reader. The researcher must be careful to report all information accurately and thoroughly and to check any details that are questionable. The investigation should seek to explore and to answer the initial research questions and should uncover all of the variables that are related to these questions.

Ary et al. (1996) contend that case studies lack breadth and that one case study may have little relevance to other settings. They mention the problems of subjectivity and prejudice in recording and interpreting case observations and emphasize the importance of rigorous testing and investigation in order to overcome these potential problems with case study research.

Interpretations

Draper (1988) suggests that 'explaining' or interpreting may include providing requested information, justifying an action, giving reasons, supporting a claim, or making a causal statement. Researchers draw their own conclusions on the basis of observations and other qualitative and quantitative data. For example, a library director may review a case study that has been written about a library employee (Mary). The case study might indicate that Mary has failed to complete assigned tasks, has not attended departmental meetings, has stolen funds from petty cash, and has claimed that she cannot lift books because of her back condition.

The director decides to check the following sources to corroborate the case study narrative. She calls Mary's supervisor and asks how many days Mary has been absent in the last three months. Mary's supervisor reports that Mary has been absent 33 days in the last three months. The director is astounded and asks if Mary has an illness. Mary's supervisor responds that she is not aware of any particular illness and also mentions that she has asked her to bring documentation to confirm her back problem. Mary has never provided any documentation from her doctor but continues to insist that she cannot lift books. Mary's supervisor also volunteered to provide the director with a specific list of tasks that she had assigned Mary a month ago and documentation that none of these tasks had been completed. The director also calls the library office administrator who confirms that on the days that Mary worked at the circulation desk, the petty cash funds did not balance. The library director also reviews copies of the minutes from Mary's department. The minutes confirm that Mary had not attended meetings for her department.

While the case study is based on direct observation, it can be considered subjective because of the researcher's bias. Corroborating case study observations with multivariate research or mixed methodologies is a major key to establishing credibility as a case study researcher. In this case, the additional documentation that Mary's supervisor and others provide serve to corroborate the case study. While it is important to provide strong supporting evidence for projects that involve large capital funding expenditures and human resources, it is even more critical that we prove our case for particularistic case studies.

Cross-case analysis

Individual case studies in general are the most common. However, aggregated groups may also be studied as cases in order to yield validity to a case theory and assertions. Cross-case analysis shows patterns and similarities among individuals within a group. For example, a researcher may choose to do a cross-case analysis of the management styles of Association of College and Research Library (ACRL) library directors. The researcher would identify common variables or traits among this group of library directors and would make appropriate assertions based on the similarities or differences among this group. This information might be helpful to trainers who are preparing training materials for these librarians or to plan curricula for schools of library and information science developing management courses.

Denzin and Lincoln (1998) suggest that looking at multiple cases in multiple settings enhances generalizability, as key processes, constructs, and explanations can be tested in many different configurations. However, there is a danger in over-generalizing in cross-case analysis. Multiple methods research is essential in accurately interpreting data that are to be generalized to a larger population.

The case study researcher may either begin a cross-case analysis with the raw data or may complete an individual case analysis for each case. The manner in which the researcher chooses to organize the data would depend on how much data is available and how the findings are to be presented.

Multiple-case data

The researcher will develop themes or categories in order to more efficiently organize the data. These themes may be derived from theoretical literature, an existing framework or schema, or the current data set.

When the researcher derives categories from the theoretical literature the intent is to provide support for a particular theory. The researcher may select themes or categories from technical literature or may use 'in vivo codes,' which are words or themes that the researcher develops based on the interviewees' own words or institutional or organizational jargon. Two commonly used frameworks are *grounded theory* and *analytical induction*.

Grounded theory involves using open coding and line-by-line analysis to dissect the data. The researcher is looking for themes within the data. Glaser and Strauss (1967) recommend applying the 'constant comparative method' in order to compare theoretical literature with the data. Open coding breaks down the data into discrete parts. Axial coding brings the data back together by making connections between the theme or category and subcategories (Strauss and Corbin, 1990). Axial coding involves identifying relationships among separate pieces of data. Axial coding may focus on conditions such as the context, actions, strategies, and consequences of actions.

Analytical induction involves using the same techniques as grounded theory. The researcher using this method formulates a theory about a situation or phenomenon and then examines the data for a fit between the theory and the actual data. The researcher continues comparing the data with the theory until a negative case is found. The purpose is to develop a theory that is sufficiently robust to handle all known cases. The researcher does not have to discard negative cases but must explain why they do not fit the theory.

When the researcher derives categories from an existing framework or schema, s/he is interested in organizing the data around an organizational framework. Sometimes this approach is used in the initial phase of data analysis to coordinate the data with program objectives and to answer key evaluation questions.

When the researcher derives categories from the current data set, s/he is trying to remain objective by setting the pre-existing data and theoretical literature aside. Russ-Eft and Preskill (2001) caution that researchers using this approach should engage more than one analyist to determine a level of inter-rater agreement.

Case-oriented analysis

There are three common approaches to case-oriented analysis: replication strategy, grounded theory applied to multiple comparison groups, and multiple exemplars applied phenomenologically. All of these approaches may potentially yield valid results. The researcher must determine which approach is most appropriate for his/her case.

Yin (1989) advocates a replication strategy. The case study researcher establishes a conceptual framework for the first case study. Successive cases are examined for similarities within this same conceptual framework. This approach is also sometimes referred to as multiple case design (Powell and Connaway, 2004). Replication logic for multiple case studies differs from sampling logic and involves carefully selecting each case to predict similar results (literal replication) or predicting contrary results for predictable reasons (theoretical replication) (Yin, 1989). For example, Mr White, a collection development librarian at Underdog University, might wish to do an analysis of his nursing collection to see if the library has a strong core nursing collection. Mr White might check with faculty in the nursing department at his institution and with bibliographic sources and conclude that the library has a strong core collection. He might then decide to do a comparative analysis of the nursing collection with a library having a similar size enrollment, in the same Carnegie class, and with a similar budget. Mr White would expect these two collections to be similar. However, Mr White's new Vice-President for Academic Affairs, Dr Wysong, is highly ambitious. Dr Wysong wants to add a nurse practitioner program. Dr Wysong attended Utopia University where she earned her undergraduate degree in nursing. She remembers the unsurpassable nursing collection that was available at Utopia University and asks Mr White to advise her of the budget that is needed to make Underdog University's nursing collection comparable to that of Utopia University.

Mr White compares database records for both institutions, he interviews the collection development librarians at Utopia University, and he talks with the faculty at Underdog University who are planning the new nurse practitioner program and distributes questionnaires for them to identify program support materials for the new program. Mr White is convinced from talking with other collection development librarians that these measures will be necessary in order to ascertain current needs, to plan for the future, and to document collection-building steps for the preliminary Nursing Board accreditation visit.

Some researchers argue that replicability is not possible because of real-world changes and the uniqueness of individuals. Marshall and Rossman (1995) conclude that researchers should allow others to inspect their procedures, protocols, and decisions by keeping all collected data in well-organized, retrievable formats.

Glaser (1978) refines the replication construct by expanding case study research to multiple comparison groups. The original case and successive cases are examined for matching variables. A new library software company, Challenger, might wish to examine troubleshooting records for the new beta version of their Challenger software. Challenger is located on the West Coast and they have heard several complaints from customers on the East Coast that they are not receiving adequate support. First, they decide to select the ten institutions from which they have received the highest number of complaints and determine that they will go to these institutions, review the problems, and interview the systems librarians at these institutions. They review their logs to determine the ten institutions that they will visit and make careful notes of the complaints at each of these institutions. They interview the ten systems librarians at these institutions, noting other problems such as climate control, user training, and systems support that may contribute to their software problems. The Challenger team then compiles the data from these ten libraries and attempts to synthesize the data, looking for commonalities and differences.

The Challenger team then decides to interview a group of ten universities on the West Coast of similar size with similar problems. They interview the ten systems librarians at these institutions, noting other problems such as climate control, user training, and systems support that may contribute to their software problems. The Challenger team then compiles the data from these ten libraries and attempts to synthesize the data looking for commonalities and differences. They note that both groups of universities are reporting similar problems but that the East Coast libraries are reporting multiple instances of the same problem because they are not receiving a timely response on problem reports logged in the mornings. They believe that the problem may be issue because their offices are open from 10–6 Pacific Time. Based on these data they are considering hiring additional morning staff from 6 to 10 a.m. Pacific Time to accommodate customers on the East Coast.

Denzin (1989) uses multiple exemplars. He looks for essential elements that may be reconstructed to address a certain phenomenon. Denzin might, for example, interview a library director that had been convicted of embezzling library funds. He might then do a number of other case studies involving library directors who have been convicted of embezzling library funds. He would then examine these studies for commonalities or multiple exemplars that might attempt to explain embezzling as a phenomenon. He would answer questions like, 'What personality traits do librarians have that embezzle money?' 'What is the socioeconomic status of the typical librarian-embezzler?' 'What are some of the reasons that the librarian-embezzler gives for committing this crime?' 'What accounting and auditing practices were practised at libraries where embezzling occurred?' 'How long had the person been embezzling funds before s/he was caught?' 'What is the typical sentence for a librarian who is convicted of embezzling funds?' Patton (1990) advocated using multiple exemplars because much can be learned from a few rich exemplars of the phenomenon in question.

Case-oriented analyses do not have to occur concurrently. A researcher may look at cases historically that have certain similarities. For example, a researcher may be planning a library director's leadership retreat. That researcher may wish to review library literature for exemplary leaders. The researcher may develop a list of criteria that apply to strong leaders in the field today and develop a matrix to apply these criteria to the group of historic library leaders. The researcher might then do a comparative analysis, examining each entity and then looking at each configuration with the case to compare variables. Similarities among and between variables help to explain cause and effect relationships.

Variable-oriented analysis

The variable-oriented approach seeks to find common themes across cases. Researchers may use matrices containing adjectives that describe management styles, quantitative measures, organizational behavior, or leadership characteristics. Variable-oriented analysis is helpful in dissecting the usefulness of different variables in a study. For example, a researcher might include educational training as a variable in a case study of ACRL library directors. The researcher might note in his/her analysis that 100 percent of the library directors that graduated from a certain university had a certain management style and consistently exhibited a specific set of management traits.

Coding the data

Case study researchers may choose to develop a system for coding their observations. For particularistic observations coding may involve making a list of the main issues and assigning numbers to each issue and then numbering each line on a page where the narrative is to be recorded. The researcher can go back and identify the line numbers from the narrative that corresponds with the issue numbers. For example, Issue 1 is that a circulation attendant says 'Get lost' to library patrons. The researcher observes the circulation attendant for a given period of time and records his/her observations. The researcher then goes back and notes the line numbers where the circulation attendant has said 'Get lost' to a library patron. He/she notes that on lines 5, 7, 11, 23, 29, 47, 53, and 81 of the report the circulation attendant has told someone to 'get lost.' Coding may involve using a tally sheet for reference questions. The main purpose of coding is for the researcher to develop a process or set of symbols that help him/her to efficiently and accurately record and report the narrative data. Coding becomes particularly important for comparative results with longitudinal case studies. It is important to establish codes and categories early on in the study in order to remain consistent throughout.

Russ-Eft and Preskill (2001) recommend the following guidelines for good category construction:

- Determine who will be involved in analyzing the qualitative data.
- Do not try to guess what respondents mean, especially on surveys.
- Make sure the categories reflect the chosen method of analysis (theoretical literature, existing framework or schema, or current data set).
- Attempt to create categories that are mutually exclusive so that a piece of data goes into one or another category but not into both.
- Keep careful notes about the decisions you make about why a certain kind of response goes in one category and not another.
- Develop a means for highlighting useful quotations you might wish to include in your final report.
- Determine what you will do with comments such as 'OK' or 'good' if they do not fit into categories.
- Develop a miscellaneous category for data that do not fit into any of the categories but that are relevant to the study's purpose.

Recording observations

Direct observations help the researcher to gain a more intense knowledge of program operations and participants' behaviors, reactions, and interactions.

Structured observations can involve inspecting or observing physical facilities as well as observing employees in a specific setting. Structured observations typically involve a preconceived notion or set of standards that are to be observed. For example, a librarian on an accreditation team may ask to see the new library addition or the new technology lab. This person might observe people interacting in these new spaces, furnishings, collections, and environmental factors such as climate control and lighting. The researcher may have a checklist of standards or criteria for conducting structured observations.

Unstructured observations may occur when an employee reacts to a comment at the water cooler or makes a passing comment in the hall. Unstructured observations are often informal opportunities that the researcher has to observe the stakeholders interacting with other participants. Unstructured observations include tone and intuition as well as direct comments. Sometimes these unstructured comments end up being tossed aside as irrelevant when the final report is composed. However, there are times when it would behoove the researcher to follow up on some of these comments at a later time with the appropriate stakeholders. Sometimes an impromptu comment may lead the researcher to request additional information or to confirm an earlier suspicion from a structured interview or observation.

The researcher's notes may be coded and categorized for later transcription. Some case study researchers do not like to be distracted with note taking while they are observing and prefer to use a tape recorder or camcorder, or have an assistant to take notes. Researchers may sometimes take photographs or draw sketches to illustrate their narrative. These media may serve to enhance the presentation but it is important to check with the department of human subjects about campus policies regarding securing appropriate permissions and to carefully adhere to these guidelines.

Site visit observations are a special category of observations according to Fitzpatrick et al. (2004). Site visits are used by most accreditation and funding agencies to evaluate a program in its naturalistic setting. Stake (1978) noted that site visits are often criticized because visitors typically only see the best sides of programs. While it is certainly the intent of most institutions to show their best side during an evaluation, the astute observer will request documentation and records that will help him/her to form a balanced picture. Fitzpatrick et al. (2004) recommend adequate preparation in order to enhance the usefulness of site visits. They specifically recommend the following activities:

1. Identifying specific information needed.

2. Developing evaluation questions to be posted during on-site interviews.

3. Developing on-site instruments (e.g. interview forms, checklists, or rating scales).

4. Selection of on-site visitor(s).

5. Pre-visit communications and arrangements.

6. Conducting the on-site evaluation visit, considering
   (a) Amount of time to be spent on site;
   (b) An initial on-site team meeting, prior to meeting with on-site administrators or staff, to reemphasize the purpose, procedures, and expected products of the visit;
   (c) An initial briefing by site administrator(s) and/or staff to orient the team to specific nuances or idiosyncratic information not readily available in pre-visit materials;
   (d) Efficient interviewing and observation by splitting the team up to cover more activities or interviewees, having the entire team together for key events or interviews with key personnel;
   (e) Interspersed team meetings to debrief and share impressions, and a final team formulation of their overall evaluation;

(f) Exit interview with the site administrator(s) and, if appropriate, site staff;

(g) Writing, disseminating, and using the final report of the on-site evaluation.

(Fitzpatrick et al., 2004: 379)

Interviews help to clarify survey information and other data. Fitzpatrick et al. (2004) differentiate between exploratory, structured, and unstructured interviews. *Exploratory interviews* are preliminary interviews that the researcher schedules with the primary stakeholders in the beginning stages of the evaluation process in order to learn about their perspectives and concerns. *Structured interviews* are planned carefully. The interviewer will ask specific questions that s/he has planned ahead of time. Structured interview questions are often follow-up questions from survey results or other data that the interviewee has previously provided. The interviewer is usually looking for specific information and will ask direct questions. *Unstructured interviews* are more general. The main goal of the interviewer in an unstructured interview is to make the interviewee feel comfortable in an effort to gain any relevant information. The interviewer may interview a student informally and ask him/her general questions about the library or a new library program in order to obtain outcomes data in a narrative form. The following general tips should be helpful in most interview situations:

1. Use professional or technical jargon only when talking to professionals.

2. Use brief questions.

3. Use supplementary materials to familiarize the interviewee with factual information before asking questions about that information. Even if the interviewee is familiar

with this information, s/he may need to see the information briefly to refresh his/her memory.

4. Use a frame of reference for complex questions. For example, if you want to know specifically about a student's opinion of the new library café, do not ask, 'What do you think about the library?'

5. Do not suggest answers. You may clarify a question or clarify a term.

6. Try to focus on the positive.

7. Interviews are not interrogations. Always attempt to make the interviewee feel at ease and encourage an open, responsive atmosphere.

Content analysis

Content analysis procedures are used to describe, analyze, and summarize trends and observations from fieldnotes and all of the data that has been collected. Content analysis involves coding and organizing data so that they may be more effectively and efficiently presented in the final report.

Quantitative content analysis would involve coding units (words and themes). A researcher might count the number of times a key word or theme appeared in a library's annual report or meeting minutes. Electronic files may be examined for quantitative data using software. Quantitative content analysis is objective and easily documented.

Qualitative content analysis would provide summaries of documents. For example, the researcher might code the library meeting minutes for the year 2006. S/he might note that the minutes for January 2006 and July 2006 dealt extensively with the new library automation software, Challenger. The researcher can then return to these notes when preparing the final report and scan the January and

July 2006 minutes where s/he has coded comments about the Challenger software as 'C-1, C-2,' etc. Miles and Huberman (1994) recommend organizing the data into topics and files, reviewing the data for causes, consequences and relationships, triangulating data with multiple sources and perspectives, developing design and evaluator checks, and recording stakeholder reactions to data and analyses.

Data analysis

Russ-Eft and Preskill (2001) recommend the following procedures for analyzing qualitative data:

- Read and reread the data. Get to know your data intimately. Compose notes or questions in the margins about what occurs to you as you read. You might highlight information that you want to go back to or use in your final report.
- Make notes (decision rules) regarding how you decide what kind of information goes in each category as well as characteristics of that category. Try out these themes with others on the evaluation team.
- Compare and contrast data with expectations, standards, or other frameworks.
- Develop codes for each category. A code is the name, acronym, or number that is associated with the category.
- Assign codes to the data.
- Sort data into the established coded categories.
- Revise codes, categories, or both as necessary.
- Whenever possible, ask a colleague to code at least a portion of the data to determine inter-rater agreement or reliability.

- Count frequency of codes, if desired.

- Look at the substance of the data within each category and examine how categories relate to each other.

- Write your findings relating them to the evaluation purpose and key questions.

- Consider displaying the data through diagrams, tables, matrices, and graphs.

- If you've also collected quantitative data, determine how you will integrate both sets of data.

- Knowing when the analysis is over is important. Though it is often tempting to keep analyzing and reanalyzing the data, you know it's time to stop when new data no longer generate new insights or there are no more data to analyze.

The case study researcher considers all of the data that have been collected. Each case analysis will include interview data, observational data, documentation data, statements and impressions. Interpreting data analyses involves organizing all of the given information and making logical conclusions from the data.

The case record organizes the raw data in a manageable form chronologically and thematically. The case study researcher is primarily concerned with analyzing the interview(s) and the observations. The researcher may write a case analysis for an interview with an individual and may also use this approach in writing about a program, group, or critical event as a single entity. The researcher will write a case study for each person interviewed or each program unit using this approach. The researcher will use a cross-case analysis to group answers from different people, groups or programs to common questions to analyze different perspectives on critical issues.

Chapter glossary

Bounding the case A term used by case study researchers to describe the context of the case. Bounding the case involves predetermining the length of time that will be committed to the case as well as human and material resources. Bounding the case involves establishing parameters for the case in the beginning.

Case context Information about the physical setting and details about the social, historical, and economic influences of the case.

Case definition The researcher should seek answers to the preliminary investigative questions regarding the case from the stakeholders and should bound or define the study using these questions.

Case expectations The researcher should provide a clear outline of the time that will be allotted for interviews, observations, and other evaluative processes at the beginning of the case study process.

Case-oriented analysis Utilizes three common approaches: *replication strategy, grounded theory applied to multiple comparison groups,* and *multiple exemplars applied phenomenologically.*

Content analysis Involves coding and organizing data so that they may be more effectively and efficiently presented in the final report.

Data analysis The case study researcher considers all of the data that have been collected. Each case analysis will include interview data, observational data, documentation data, statements, and impressions. Data analysis involves organizing all of the given information and making logical conclusions from the data.

Exploratory interviews Preliminary interviews that the researcher schedules with the primary stakeholders in the beginning stages of the evaluation process in order to learn about their perspectives and concerns.

Foreshadowing Foreshadowing involves providing sufficient background information on the case to sufficiently ground it within the literature and other relevant contexts.

Grounded theory applied to multiple comparison groups The original case and successive cases are examined for matching variables.

Instrumentation The research strategy that is used to report the case study results.

Interpretations Interpreting may include providing requested information, justifying an action, giving reasons, supporting a claim, or making a causal statement. Researchers draw their own conclusions on the basis of observations and other qualitative and quantitative data.

Investigating The case study researcher must provide information to substantiate a claim or problem, and to instruct, inform, or motivate the reader. The investigation should seek to explore and to answer the initial research questions and should uncover all of the variables that are related to these questions.

Multiple-case data The researcher may use several cases in order to validate results. When using multiple cases, the researcher will develop themes or categories in order to more efficiently organize the data. These themes may be derived from theoretical literature, an existing framework or schema, or the current data set.

Multiple exemplars applied phenomenologically The case study researcher looks for essential elements that may be reconstructed to address a certain phenomenon.

Replication strategy The case study researcher establishes a conceptual framework for the first case study.

Successive cases are examined for similarities within this same conceptual framework.

Research questions Research questions may be used initially as hypothesis statements. They will be used throughout the study to provide focus and clarity for the researcher and for the stakeholders.

Sampling Sampling involves selecting critical cases, extreme cases, typical cases, and varied cases. The logic and power of probability sampling depends on selecting a random and statistically representative sample that will justify generalizations to a larger population. However, the power and logic of purposeful sampling lies in selecting information-rich cases for in-depth study.

Site visit observations Site visits are used by most accreditation and funding agencies to evaluate a program in its naturalistic setting.

Structured interview questions Usually structured interview questions are follow-up questions from survey results or other data that the interviewee has previously provided. The interviewer is usually looking for specific information and will ask direct questions.

Structured observations Typically involve a preconceived notion or set of standards that are to be observed.

Unstructured interviews The main goal of the interviewer in an unstructured interview is to make the interviewee feel comfortable in an effort to gain any relevant information.

Variable-oriented analysis The variable-oriented approach seeks to find common themes across cases. Researchers may use matrices containing adjectives that describe management styles, quantitative measures, organizational behavior, or leadership characteristics.

Focus questions

1. What are your research questions?

2. How would you define your problem or case?

3. What are your case expectations?

4. What case study sampling techniques do you intend to use?

5. How will you code your data?

Application exercises

1. Describe your case context.

2. Define your case problem or case.

3. Outline your case study strategy.

References and further reading

Ary, D., Jacobs, L., and Razavieh, A. (1996) *Introduction to Research in Education,* 5th edn. Fort Worth, TX: Harcourt Brace.

Binnendijk, A. (1986) *AID's Experience with Contraceptive Social Marketing: A Synthesis of Project Evaluation Findings,* AID Evaluation Special Study No. 40. Washington, DC: US Agency for International Development.

Bremer, J., Cole, E., Irelan, W. and Rourk, P. (1985) *A Review of AID's Experience in Private Sector Development,* AID Program Evaluation Report No. 14. Washington, DC: US Agency for International Development.

Chew, S. (1989) *Agroforestry Projects for Small Farmers,*

AID Evaluation Special Study No. 59. Washington, DC: US Agency for International Development.

Denzin, N. (1989) *Interpretive Biography*, Qualitative Research Methods, 17. Thousand Oaks, CA : Sage.

Denzin, N. and Lincoln, Y. (1998) *Collecting and Interpreting Qualitative Materials.* Thousand Oaks, CA: Sage.

Draper, S. (1988) 'What's going on in everyday explanation?', in C. Antaki (ed.), *Analyzing Everyday Explanations: A Casebook of Methods.* Newbury Park, CA: Sage, pp. 15–31.

Fitzpatrick, J., Sanders, J., and Worthen, B. (2004) *Program Evaluation: Alternative Approaches and Practical Guidelines*, 3rd edn, Boston: Allyn & Bacon.

Glaser, B. and Strauss, A. (1967) *Discovery of Grounded Theory: Strategies for Qualitative Research.* Chicago: Aldine.

Glaser, E. (1978) *Theoretical Sensitivity.* Mill Valley, CA: Sociology Press.

Johnston, B., Hoben, A., Dijkerman, D., and Jaeger, W. (1987) *An Assessment of AID Activities to Promote Agricultural and Rural Development in Sub-Saharan Africa*, AID Evaluation Special Study No. 54. Washington, DC: US Agency for International Development.

Kanter, R. M. (1983) *The Change Masters: Innovation for Productivity in the American Corporation.* New York: Simon & Schuster.

Marshall, C. and Rossman, G. (1995) *Designing Qualitative Research,* 2nd edn, Thousand Oaks, CA: Sage.

Miles, M. and Huberman, A. (1994) *Qualitative Data Analysis.* Thousand Oaks, CA: Sage.

Parlett, M. and Hamilton, D. (1976) 'Evaluation as

illumination: a new approach to the study of innovatory programs,' in G.V. Glass (ed.), *Evaluation Studies Review Annual*, Vol. 1. Beverly Hills, CA: Sage.

Patton, M. (1990) *Qualitative Evaluation and Research Methods*, 2nd edn. Newbury Park, CA: Sage.

Patton, M. (2002) *Qualitative Research and Evaluation Methods*. Thousand Oaks, CA: Sage.

Peshkin, A. (1988) 'In search of subjectivity – one's own', *Educational Researcher*, 17 (7): 17–22.

Peters, T. and Waterman, R. Jr (1982) *In Search of Excellence: Lessons from America's Best-run Companies*. New York: Harper & Row.

Powell, R. and Connaway, L. (2004) *Basic Research Methods for Librarians*, 4th edn, Library and Information Science Text Series. Westport, CT: Libraries Unlimited.

Rogers, B. and Wallerstein, M. (1985) *PL 480 Title I: Impact Evaluation Results and Recommendations*, AID Program Evaluation Report No. 13. Washington, DC: US Agency for International Development.

Russ-Eft, D. and Preskill, H. (2001) *Evaluation in Organizations*. Cambridge, MA: Perseus.

Stake, R. (1978) *The Case Study Method in Social Inquiry*. Thousand Oaks, CA: Sage.

Stake, R. (1995) *The Art of Case Study Research*. Thousand Oaks, CA: Sage.

Steinberg, D. (1983) *Irrigation and AID's Experience: A Consideration Based on Evaluation*, AID Evaluation Special Study No. 8. Washington, DC: US Agency for International Development.

Strauss, A. and Corbin, J. (1994) *Basics of Qualitative Research: Grounded Theory Procedures and Techniques*. Thousand Oaks: Sage.

Tilney, J., Jr and Riordan, J. (1988) *Agricultural Policy*

Analysis and Planning: A Summary of Two Recent Analyses of AID-Supported Projects Worldwide, AID Evaluation Special Study No. 55. Washington, DC: US Agency for International Development.

Warren, M. (1984) *AID and Evaluation: A Sector Report on Lessons Learned*, AID Program Evaluation Report No. 12. Washington, DC: US Agency for International Development.

Wasserman, G. and Davenport, A. (1983) *Power to the People: Rural Electrification Sector Summary Report*, AID Program Evaluation Report No. 11. Washington, DC: US Agency for International Development.

Yin, R. (1989) *Case Study Research: Design and Methods*, rev. edn. Newbury Park, CA: Sage.

Utilizing the case study approach for program evaluation

Ravonne A. Green

This book focuses on case studies as part of just-in-time (JIT) management. JIT management constantly requires making decisions that involve evaluating programs and processes. While individual case studies are useful for instructional purposes, the greater need in most library settings is for narrative accounts to document outcomes in support of a program.

A case study is included in this chapter as an illustration that utilizes a multiple-methods approach. This case illustrates guidelines, application strategies, and design techniques. Even though this case study provides details for a comprehensive program evaluation, the cycle may be adapted as needed to support local program assessment needs. Similar methods may also be used for individual or instrumental case studies.

This case study describes the information competency curriculum evaluation at South Central University, a mythical institution. I have chosen to use a multiple-methods approach because it provides the most thorough level of data analysis. I have recorded the case in first-person form. This is typical of many case studies; however, it is not always necessary to use first-person language.

This study is written as a first-person account and the author is selected to conduct the case study analysis because of her national recognition in the area of information competency, her familiarity with similar programs, and her strong background in assessment. These are not necessarily my strengths. They are strengths that a consultant for a study of this nature should possess.

This case study involves inviting an outside consultant. There are situations, however, when it is appropriate for an insider to conduct a study such as the one described here. It is best to ask someone outside the library to assist with the collection of data and the writing of the report in order to guarantee objectivity, to gain a deeper perspective, and to ensure inter-rater reliability. This approach should work in any library setting by assembling a committee of professionals either internally or externally to accomplish the appropriate tasks.

The South Central University Information Competency Curriculum

I had met Jason Walters at the Association of College and Research Librarians (ACRL) conference last spring. Jason was a reference librarian at South Central University. He had attended a panel discussion that I participated in about integrating information literacy skills into the higher education curriculum. Jason came up to talk to me after the session. He was proud of the information competency program that he and his colleagues had developed at South Central. Jason's enthusiasm was infectious as he talked about the amazing results that he had seen in the brief pilot period that the course had been offered. Jason paused at one point and said:

> There is one problem. As I mentioned, this is a four-year pilot and some of the faculty members are highly opposed to adding another three-credit hour course to the curriculum. That is why I wanted to talk to you. I don't know much about assessment and besides the provost has said that she needs to see something more than a survey. Is there any way that you would be willing to come and help us? We just need to know how to pull the data together and how to convince the faculty that this program is worth while. We would like for someone to come from outside just to go over the data that we have collected and to help to make things more convincing.

I asked Jason to have his library director contact me. Dr Jane Walters, the library director at South Central, did so the following week. She had already spoken with the provost at South Central about the evaluation. Dr Porter, the provost, had indicated that she would approve a visit from an outside evaluator. Dr Walters was contacting me to request that I send a proposal.

I submitted the proposal addressing the topics that Dr Walters had mentioned in her conversation with me. Dr Walters called me a few weeks later and informed me that my proposal had been accepted and we set up a date for me to visit South Central.

The provost, Dr Anne Porter, met me at the door of the administration building at South Central University. Dr Porter invited me to her office and began to chat briefly about the information competency curriculum. She made it clear that she wanted an objective evaluation of the new information competency curriculum.

> I know you may have visited other universities with better programs. We are very proud of the program that we have here but there is always room for improvement. In addition to suggesting improvements, I have to tell you that this program has been highly controversial on our campus. While we have had some perceived gains in academic achievement as a result of this program, this is a required three-credit hour course. Many faculty members question the logic of adding another three-credit hour course to the core curriculum when our number of core requirements is already higher than any other state university.

Dr Porter then produced an agenda for meetings with individuals over the next few days. I would spend the next two days interviewing the library director and the reference librarians that were involved in teaching the course. On Thursday I would meet with faculty members that had collaborated with the librarians in developing the information competency course. On Thursday afternoon and Friday I would meet with individual students that had completed the course. On the following Monday, I would attend a faculty meeting in which the librarians were going to make a presentation based on an assessment that they had completed at the end of the course. There would be a question and answer session at the end of this meeting for the librarians to address lingering concerns about the program. I would then wrap up meetings with the library staff and with the provost. I would contact any of the stakeholders after I returned home with questions about my data and to confirm my research. I would send the library director and the provost a draft copy of my study within two weeks to be distributed to appropriate stakeholders. I would return a month later to make a presentation from my data to the Academic Affairs Committee. There would be a brief discussion about the program and then a vote would be taken to determine the fate of the information competency program at South Central University.

Codes

I established a list of codes for my fieldnotes before going to South Central:

F – Faculty
S – Students
SS – Support Staff
A – Administrators

Documents

I contacted Jason and requested the following documents prior to my arrival:

- the survey that Jason had mentioned when I saw him at ACRL;
- the pre- and post-test scores from the information competency course;
- LibQUAL results for South Central and their benchmark group;
- access to the information competency course website so that I could review student papers and projects;
- copies of the information competency course evaluations;
- copies of the information competency reflection papers;

- a copy of the original course proposal;
- a list of all of the faculty, administrators, and support staff that had been involved with developing and teaching the information competency course with comments about the particular sections of the course that they developed or taught.

I contacted Dr Sanders, the director of institutional research, and requested a copy of a study that he had done with retention data from the cohort that had completed the information competency course.

I contacted Dr Anderson, the dean of student services and requested a copy of a study that her department had conducted among students with learning disabilities that had completed the information competency course. This study involved grade point average data, retention comments, and brief interviews.

Triangulation

I immersed myself in the literature on integrating information competency into the higher education curriculum. I reviewed the ACRL Information Literacy Standards. I read Teresa Neely's book, *Information Literacy Assessment* (Chicago: ALA, 2006) and Ilene Rockman's book, *Integrating Information Literacy into the Higher Education Curriculum: Practical Models for Transformation* (San Francisco: Jossey-Bass, 2004). I also read numerous professional journal articles and books on this topic. I developed a list of terms and a corresponding matrix. I asked several librarian colleagues who had recently published in this area if they would be willing to share their curricula, assessment tools, and information literacy website URLs with me. I reviewed library information literacy websites for colleges in Jason's state. I checked with the director of institutional research at South Central and asked for a list of their benchmark institutions. I compared information literacy programs for these institutions and requested assessments.

I requested interviews with all of the librarians and faculty that had been involved with developing and teaching the information competency course. I wanted to get a sense from them about the environment, student achievement, and their individual notion about the utility of the course.

After reviewing the pre- and post-test scores, student papers and projects, I selected 20 students to conduct individual interviews with based on their exemplary work and test score gains. I developed a brief list of interview questions and sent these to Jason for review and asked him to test the interview questions on a pilot group of students.

I enlisted the help of the director of institutional research in planning a focus group session that I would conduct while I was on campus. We discussed methodologies and specific items. Dr Sanders spoke with the library director and they agreed to invite a reference librarian from another library with a similar program to conduct the focus group to ensure anonymity and objectivity.

I contacted the dean of student support services concerning the data that she had collected and we decided to collaborate on a follow-up questionnaire. I sent her a pilot copy that she distributed to three students that had participated in her study. She administered the pilot version and returned it to me to clarify a couple of items. We would have a pizza party and invite all of the students to complete the questionnaire while I was on campus.

I would use all of these data to provide the faculty at South Central University with an accurate analysis of the information literacy program. This was going to be an intense week. My goal was to go into the project as an informed professional and to properly inform other professionals about the outcomes of the information competency course.

Part 2

Valdosta State University student case studies

Case studies involve observing and assessing programs and individuals within programs. There are many facets to any case. As professionals we can write case studies based on a real or perceived library problem and allow staff members the opportunity to brainstorm possible solutions in an objective manner. It is amazing how many solutions one group of people can produce in a relatively short time.

Librarians are good storytellers but case studies are more than just good stories. A good case study does not just present a problem but asks questions that point toward documentation. A good case study has universality and can be applied in more than one setting.

The following case studies are based on actual dilemmas that these students have faced or cases that were reported to them by practising librarians. There are questions that might help you to apply these cases in your own library. There are analyses provided by other students in the class. These analyses represent one way of viewing or resolving the case. The solutions that are given are not the only solutions. I have never heard two people agree on how a case should be resolved. That is one of the things that make case studies so interesting. You will come to different conclusions as you read these cases. There are no right and wrong answers.

Reading and writing case studies forces us to think outside the box. As you read these case studies, you will begin to think more globally about your library problems. Case studies invite team work. The old cliché 'two heads are better than one' most definitely applies to solving library problems and evaluating library programs.

Possible alternative scenarios are suggested for some case studies. These exercises are intended to inspire continued thought and to reinforce effective problem-solving skills.

Special funding: use it or lose it

Wendell C. Stone

Introduction

A new university library director faces a dilemma involving a renovation grant that her library has been awarded. She must decide whether she can meet the criteria and deadline imposed by the grant with the available staff and resources.

The case

On 1 July 2005, Carolyn Flannigan assumed the position of Director of University Libraries of East Central University, leaving her position as Associate University Librarian and Professor of Library Science at East Central University. At East Central University, she replaced Carl Johnson, a popular figure who had led the library from August 1978 through May 2004 when his health forced him to retire. He died shortly after his retirement. In nearly 30 years service to East Central Library, Johnson developed a notable reputation on campus, leading the library through a period of enormous change as the card catalog was replaced by an electronic system, GALILEO was introduced, and the university saw rapid expansion. In addition to his prominent role on East Central University's campus, Johnson also held influential positions in various state and regional organizations. Replacing such a figure was a challenge in itself; the challenge soon became even greater for Flannigan.

To the extent that she had been able to develop a routine in her short service at East Central Library, it was on a routine day in fall semester when she sat down to check her mail. As she browsed through the incoming correspondence, she reached a letter that held surprising news and that started a sequence of events that were anything but routine. The letter announced that the library had been awarded about $120,000 in Minor Repair and Renovation (MRR) money to expand the facilities housing the Fannie Mae Winters Special Collection. Unaware that a request for the funds had been made, Flannigan searched through the files of the prior director to find further information on the project. When she found no reference to it, she consulted with John Mandira, the Associate Director of University Libraries, and Stacy Martin, Special Collections Librarian. Neither of these individuals had heard about the project. In fact, no one in the library seemed to know much, if anything, about it. In retrospect, it seems that the request for the funds was made orally by Carl Johnson. Johnson had been ill during his last few weeks of employment with East Central University – so much so that he could not even attend his own retirement party. It appears that documentation of the request for funds had been overlooked during this period of illness and transition, thus not leaving a paper trail for current library staff to follow.

The need for expanding the special collections area has been clear for some time. During the first 75 years of its existence, East Central University had not maintained a special collections area. In 1980, Johnson secured funding for starting a special collection program and hired Stacy Martin to oversee it. Much of Martin's initial efforts were focused on gathering material that either related to the history of the university or supported its programs and services. Currently, the mission of the Fannie Mae Winters Special Collection identifies five areas of interest:

- the history of the East Central University;
- the university's curriculum;
- the East Central University area;
- sacred harp music; and
- rare books.

In recent years, the library has secured a large collection of material related to politicians in the East Central University area, including significant collections donated by two state senators. Their largest single collection is that donated by a former congressman and his colleagues. This recent influx of materials meant that the special collections had exceeded its storage to the extent that many items had been stored in the basement of the library. Furthermore, the security and safety of documents has been compromised by the lack of a reading room designated specifically for special collections. The new construction would enclose an additional 2,100 square feet to be used both for storage and as a reading room.

Thus when Flannigan opened the letter announcing the award, she was both excited and relieved until she read the stipulations. Then she became a bit concerned, particularly by two requirements:

1. All funds had to be expended by the end of the fiscal year.
2. The funding maximum was inflexible.

77

The library would lose the money if construction and its related expenses could not be completed within the year or if no bid came in within the amount that had been funded. The library staff would have to determine the precise configuration they wanted, obtain architectural drawings, secure bids for the work, clear the space to be enclosed, obtain required permits, and oversee the completion of the construction in less than a year. Normally, this work would proceed rather methodically, in a step-by-step fashion. The rigid timeframe, however, meant that the work had to be compressed. For example, clearing the space for the expansion had to begin as soon as possible to ensure no delay in construction.

The location of the expansion was on the third floor of the library, in an area in which 13 desks, 65 chairs, and a good many shelves of books were housed. Most of the books were adult or juvenile fiction, left over from the early years in the library's history when fiction had been segregated from other materials. For some time, cataloging staff had been working on recataloging fiction, but had completed well under half of it. There was no space in the building to which these items could simply be moved with the order retained so that the recataloging could continue, as it had before, on a time-available basis. Instead, the fiction would have to be removed from the shelves until it could be reclassified. To get the material back on the shelves within a reasonable time, Flannigan would have to add a temporary staff line to an already overstretched budget. While architectural drawings were in process and bids were being accepted, staff would have to begin the process of weeding, recataloging, and reshelving materials located in the potential construction site, as well as resituating desks and other furniture. The library could very possibly make quite a large investment of its personnel and financial resources only to find that the project failed because of excessive costs or because of contractors' inability to meet the deadlines. In that case, not only would library personnel have wasted precious resources, but they would also have created a large vacant area with nothing to put back into it.

An additional issue faced by library staff in considering the construction was that no funds were allocated for furnishing the new space. Furthermore, given the continually shrinking library budget, no funds would be available from regular sources for purchasing the necessary items. The storage area would need little in this regard, but the reading room would need all new furniture, particularly if it was (as hoped) going to serve as both a reading room and much needed classroom space. Potentially, then, the library could end up with a reading/classroom that was at best filled with cast-off items from other areas of the university or, more probably, totally empty (and thus hardly useful for either reading or teaching).

To further complicate matters, the building housing East Central Library had begun to show its age. The electrical system was approaching overload and the interior of the building needed extensive renovation. Though no new capital projects would be funded before 2012, Flannigan and her staff had begun developing plans to ensure that the library received consideration for renovation when money for major building projects became available. Not only did the current state of the building limit expansion, but the entire building could face extensive renovation within less than ten years.

The $120,000 in MRR funds awarded to the library posed risks and challenges even for an established director. For a person who had been in charge for only weeks and who had not yet proven herself in the position, the risks and challenges became even greater.

Case study analysis

Alberta Ruth Hayden

I have selected Wendell C. Stone's special collections expansion case study for analysis and will suggest alternative solutions to solve this unusual dilemma and also suggest an implementation plan. I will be following the steps outlined in *A Model for Case Analysis and Problem Solving* prepared by Prof. Edward G. Wertheim at Northeastern University.

Comprehend the case situation: collect data, identify relevant facts

The East Central University Library has received notification of a $120,000 award for repairs and renovation to the facility housing the Fannie Mae Winters Special Collection. The security and storage of the growing collection has been an ongoing problem, and there is no reading room for patrons to use. Acceptance of the funds would necessitate a significant amount of unbudgeted expenditures, staff time, and reshuffling of priorities. If the project cannot be completed in time and within budget, the money will be withdrawn.

Define the problem

The problem is whether the newly hired director should proceed with accepting a $120,000 Minor Repair and Renovation award because of the multiple restrictions and risks involved, including space, furniture, construction, and costs incurred. Without benefit of the previous director's written correspondence and rationale, the new director has no background information with which to proceed. There are significant financial investments to be committed by the library. There are significant staffing investments to be committed by the library. There are significant bidding and construction deadlines that must be met by sources outside the immediate control of the director. Finally, the director does not know whether this financial investment will be affected by the long-term plans for major building renovation.

Generating alternative solutions/implementing a plan and following up

There are several areas the director should investigate prior to committing to accepting the funds. A great deal of additional information is needed before a decision can be made whether or not to accept the funds.

First, she should seek out professional assistance in making this decision. The associate director, university librarians, and the special collections librarian should become part of the decision-making team. The university's building and maintenance director should be consulted. The team should determine if (a) the award is worth the expenditures and (b) if it's fiscally possible to meet the construction deadline restrictions.

Second, the director should call the benefactors providing the award and discuss with them the stipulations as presented. She should ask about the rigidity of the deadlines and requirements. If the director anticipates the project could take longer than the deadline, she should outline these concerns with her contact before accepting the funds. She should find out to what degree the donors will work with the library if unexpected delays should occur. The director should attempt to create a positive working relationship with her MRR contact. The director, through her network of professional contacts, should find out who else has received this award and discuss their experiences (success and failure) with similar projects, including their timelines and expenditures.

If the director determines that a feasible plan can be implemented, she should seek additional funds from other sources to supplement this plan, perhaps tapping a university donor to furnish the reading room, volunteers who can be trained for the re-cataloging effort or asking the university trustees to allocate additional funds for staff and construction.

Should the funds be accepted, a detailed implementation plan should be written and followed. If the director believes she will be unable to monitor the project herself on a day-to-day basis due to her other responsibilities, she should assign the daily coordination of this project to an experienced staff member. Her active involvement will be necessary throughout the project.

Alternative scenarios

Write an analysis of the case study as it is presented or select one of the following scenarios, write an analysis, and suggest a possible solution.

1. Ms Flannigan receives a second letter from the Development Office stating that Mr Johnson had agreed to match the funds that were to be allocated to provide adequate shelving and other materials for the new special collections area. Mr Johnson's estate will remain in

probate for one year. Mr Johnson suffered from a terminal illness that involved expensive medical treatments. It is doubtful that there were any funds left in his estate. No one knows if Mr Johnson had included the library in his will. Ms Flannigan has already hired an architect. The drawings have been completed and approved by the Board of Regents. The contractor has been hired and has been paid his first construction draw.

2. Ms Flannigan receives a phone call from the Development Office at East Central University regarding a prominent politician who had donated his papers to the library the last year that Mr Johnson served as director. Mr Johnson had promised him that he would digitize all of his papers and develop a link to his papers from the library website. The politician had pledged a million dollar gift to the library for the special collections expansion project. Mr Johnson had not left any correspondence about this gift and Stacy Martin, the special collections librarian, had not been apprised of this situation. The politician insisted that unless the papers were digitized by 15 September, he would come and take them back. The public must have access to his papers before the November election, he insisted. It is 23 July and there are no staff members who have the time or expertise to accomplish this task in this limited amount of time. The director of development insisted that Ms Flannigan should somehow manage to get the congressman's papers digitized by the deadline because it would be bad public relations not to accommodate his request. Ms Flannigan must also manage the building project and there are no university funds for hiring additional staff.

Discussion questions

1. Should Ms Flannigan accept the MRR funds? Why or why not?

2. How should Ms Flannigan organize or manage this project?

Employee training

Christopher Sharpe

Introduction

A full-time evening employee at a university library is confused about her level of authority and frustrated by the lack of professional development opportunities. Her work hours give her little contact with other library workers and she does not have much involvement in library activities beyond her circulation desk duties. She likes the university atmosphere, but she feels that she has not accomplished much in her ten years at the library.

The case

Lisa* has worked at Hunter University* for about ten years, and she is a paraprofessional assigned to the circulation desk. She is now in her fifties and has a husband and two children. She was an elementary school teacher in her twenties, but became a homemaker when she had her first child. She worked a few clerical jobs when her two children got a little older. Ten years ago she got a full-time paraprofessional position at the Hunter library working in microfilm and at the circulation desk.

Hunter University has about 20,000 students and a small library staff of 30. Paraprofessional jobs are few and far between. Five years ago, the reserves staff member left Hunter to work in another library and Lisa thought that she would like to apply for that position. But soon Mary,* a staff member in her twenties, told the administrators and others that she would like to be the new reserves coordinator. Lisa does not like conflict, and believed the administrators were set on Mary, and so she did not apply for the job. She has regretted that decision and wished that she had at least applied for the position.

A few years later, the evening circulation position opened up and Lisa applied and got the job. Lisa's children were all in college, and she was always a bit of a night-owl, so the position was well suited for her. Along with closing the library at midnight, the job includes the responsibility of making the night student assistants' schedule.

She likes some of the aspects of her position; it gives her time to run errands in the mornings and the library is usually less busy at night. But she has discovered some drawbacks: policy decisions or discussions occur in the morning or afternoon before Lisa arrives, and so she is usually the last person notified of changes. She is usually notified through e-mail, by means of notes, or if another staff member remembers to tell her. Sometimes she is not even told of changes or they may be complicated, but those who made the changes usually leave by 5 p.m.

There have also been occasions when Lisa was the only person closing the library. A late night reference librarian was hired over a year ago, but before that Lisa had to answer reference questions and handle circulation issues on her own or with a student assistant. There have been times when student assistants were not available or have called in sick. If she is alone, Lisa calls the campus police to let them know of her situation in case she needs their help.

Lisa is not clear about what authority she has at night. She makes the student assistant schedule after 5 p.m. but there have been times when some student assistants' schedules have already been made up to their end time at 7 p.m. There have been some minor conflicts about the way she has scheduled some students. Lisa believes that the student assistant supervisor just changes the student assistant schedule to suit them (for example, moving their hours from night to mostly day time) and rarely consults with Lisa about these schedule changes.

Lisa is frustrated with the feeling that she is stuck in her position with no chance at advancement or professional improvement. Also, when she decides to take vacation or sick leave, it can be very troublesome for the supervisors to rearrange schedules or find someone to close those nights. The new late night reference librarian helps, but the supervisors try to call in another staff member or student assistant to help him close if Lisa has the night off. Yet when Lisa finds that she is on her own for the night the supervisors do not call in help for her.

Lisa has also arrived at work and noticed that a library conference had occurred that day. She is frustrated that she never sees an announcement for these events and that it always seems to be the same people attending since she started work at the library. She's never been asked to join any committee (the few that exist) and has not received any additional training. Recently, Lisa has noticed that another paraprofessional receives training on Interlibrary Loan requests. 'Why don't they offer this training to me?' she wonders.

Although the pay may be low and she is frustrated with the lack of professional advancement, Lisa does not want to leave the library. Her home is nearby and she likes the university setting. Yet, when she looks back on her career at Hunter, she feels that her job duties and responsibilities have not changed much. Lisa hopes there will be some changes in the library in the next few years, but considering that most people in management have been there for about ten years she is not expecting anything.

* *Names and some personal facts changed to respect privacy.*

Case study analysis

Sammy Dees

This situation shows a lack of professionalism on the part of Hunter University's head librarian and a need for 'Lisa' to become more assertive and stand up for her rights.

First, despite the fact that Lisa's job is at night, it is no less important than day jobs. The fact that Lisa let a position that she really wanted, the reserves coordinator position, pass by without even applying shows she must have a low self-esteem or feels less important than other employees.

Lisa's quiet demeanor has apparently led the other employees to believe that she is a 'pushover' and will not do anything to make a fuss or push the limit.

Lisa should request a written job description. She should make a chart of what her job requires and outline how she completes each component of the job. Then she should make an appointment with the library director for a consultation. She should point out how she has not been advised of meetings, changes, and workshops. She should discuss the fact that she has been in situations where she needed to respond to challenging reference questions but has never been trained to work at the reference desk. She has been left to manage the library and to be responsible for maintaining a safe and secure environment at night. She should make known the fact that she has seniority and that her job is being overridden by students changing their schedules and not informing her of these changes. In essence, her job is being compromised.

She should ask the director to address each of these concerns and ask for a date when she may come back for answers to her concerns and what directives the director has for solving these problems. In the interim, she should send a letter documenting this meeting to the director of human resources at the university, so that he/she could be kept abreast of the problems and concerns Lisa has about her job. She should also send copies of her performance evaluations to document the glowing comments about her responsible, dedicated service.

After all of this done, if nothing has changed, then perhaps a meeting needs to be arranged with human resources and the library director for Lisa to outline her options. If she really likes her job, then her determination for equality should be evident. If she makes enough 'noise,' then something should be done, or other options such as grievances or litigation could be considered to make the powers-that-be aware that she has backbone, integrity, and fight.

Case study analysis

Alberta Ruth Hayden

I have selected Chris Sharpe's case study for analysis and will suggest the most viable (in my opinion) alternatives for

Lisa to take to resolve her myriad of problems and also suggest an implementation plan. I will be following the steps outlined in *A Model for Case Analysis and Problem Solving* prepared by Prof. Edward G. Wertheim at Northeastern University.

Comprehend the case situation: collect data, identify relevant facts

Lisa, a paraprofessional, works at the Hunter library as the evening circulation staff member. Lisa has been in this position for ten years and has limited supervisory responsibilities. She has limited contact with supervisors and co-workers.

Define the problem

Lisa enjoys the flexibility of working evenings because this shift best suits her personal schedule and also the library is less busy at night. She feels frustrated with her lack of career movement and her perceived lack of influence/power, and is dismayed by the lack of concern by decision-makers within her work environment about issues that concern her, particularly staffing and safety issues in the late evening. Lisa does not want to leave her position but does not see the situation improving in the near future. She is concerned about her future career growth opportunities as well as the day-to-day problems in her current situation.

Lisa's position appears to be stable and since she has been in this situation for an extended period of time there seems to be no urgency to solve this problem immediately (other than personal desire). It is not known what Lisa's annual reviews have indicated as to her performance versus supervisor expectations. It is not known what Lisa's relationships are with her co-workers and her supervisor. It is not known if Lisa's problems are isolated or are indicative of a system-wide situation.

Causes

There appear to be multiple causes for these problems.

1. Lisa works during a timeframe when decision-makers are not available for consultation and so her access is limited.

2. Lisa has not previously made proactive moves to outline her concerns.

3. An environment does not exist that would encourage Lisa's involvement and feedback about her work concerns.

4. Lisa does not seem to have a network of co-workers to support her efforts and keep her informed about upcoming events, activities, and opportunities.

5. Lisa has not taken proactive movements to move into another position that might improve her situation.

Generating alternative solutions/implementing a plan and following up

There are several solutions that might work individually or in concert with each other.

1. Lisa should make her professional needs known to decision-makers. She needs to create opportunities to 'network' and become visible to supervisors who can influence her career movement. Lisa can accomplish this

by volunteering for special projects, preparing and presenting memos with suggestions for improvements, and making verbal and written efforts that identify her as a problem-solver rather than a problem herself.

2. Lisa should apply for other positions that would allow her to work when training and professional development is offered.

3. Lisa should make written requests to attend training sessions regardless of when they are scheduled. She can also request to be put on the e-mail list for training.

4. Lisa should approach her supervisor specifically requesting help in determining the limits of her authority. If others exceed their authority, Lisa should speak with them and then bring the situation to her supervisor if the issues continue.

5. Although the case study does not specifically mention the results of Lisa's yearly performance review, this is a key to her growth and success. Lisa's work history as presented does not show her to be an assertive team player. If this has been noted in her Reviews, improvements must be made on Lisa's part so that she can be considered for promotions or movement within the paraprofessional arena.

6. Lisa should determine what if any written policy exists regarding one person being alone in the building. There are safety and insurance issues involved, and she should bring this problem to the attention of multiple decision-makers.

7. Lisa can also show her interest in career opportunities by beginning an MLIS degree program. That will surely get management's attention. The classes she takes in library school will also give her a broad perspective of what life

is like for the decision-makers who 'usually leave by 5 p.m.' I think Lisa would be surprised to see that their time is booked full of issues that she does not need to address during the evenings but are critical to the overall performance of the library. Working on an advanced degree will also help Lisa's frustration with career stagnation.

8. Lisa can also choose not to do anything. She can decide if the benefits of the position are worth the frustrations. She can decide if the ramifications involved in implementing a career action plan will be worth the conflicts, personal energy, and effort involved.

Case study analysis

Maradith H. Sheffield and Julia Huprich

Comprehend the case situation: collect data, identify relevant facts

Lisa is the night administrator at the Hunter University Library. She has been working there for ten years. She enjoys her job and its proximity to her home. However, she is concerned about career advancement and other communication issues on the job. Lisa is experiencing four key issues:

1. *Lack of goal-setting.* Lisa's supervisor should help her identify her goals, whether they are for advancement or other areas of professional development.

2. *Communication issues.* A solution should be recommended for this issue. Lisa is often unaware of policy changes and dates of meetings.

3. *Lack of understanding about authority.* An official job description should be identified for Lisa

4. *Lack of personnel support.* Lisa is left alone at closing time.

All four issues need to be addressed for Lisa to be a happy, productive employee.

Causes

1. Lisa has been working for ten years. According to McClelland's need theory, a worker has a need for achievement: a drive to excel. Lisa feels the need for improvement.

2. Communication between Lisa and daytime administrators and staff is poor to say the least. Sporadic e-mails and hoping that a staff member will 'remember' to tell her of policy changes is not a dependable system of communication.

3. Lisa was not given a clear job description. She was forced to do the work of several employees. On occasion she has had to handle reference questions and circulation issues among her other duties. When she makes out student work schedules, they are sometimes changed by day management.

4. Lisa is often the only person working the late hours in the library. Even though the library is not busy at night, Lisa should not be left alone to close at midnight.

Generating alternative solutions/ implementing a plan and following up

1. Lisa could begin by talking with her direct supervisor. She should go to her supervisor and express her concerns. Let him/her know that she is concerned about career advancement, concerned about her amount of authority in the library at night, and talk about the lack of communication. It may be possible that her supervisor does not realize what is going on and needs to be made aware of the situation.

2. Lisa could put her concerns in writing. She could write a memo or letter to her supervisor expressing her concerns and asking for help with the issues. Making the person in the line of command aware of the situation is always a good choice.

3. Lisa could begin asking for dates and times of important meetings. She could do this by coming in to work early each day or by initiating the e-mails concerning meetings to ask for dates and times. Maybe this would help her to attend more of the policy changing meetings and allow her to be more in tune with the other administrators and with changes in the library. She would then be able to talk with others about their training and keep up with upcoming opportunities. She should also talk to her supervisor to communicate her concern about missing meetings and other professional opportunities.

4. Lisa could go directly to the library director. She could take her concerns to the director verbally or in written format. Either way, she would need to explain all of her concerns and ask for help resolving each.

5. Lisa should check policies and procedures to see what it says about closing the library. Most businesses require

two people to lock up, especially so late at night. This should be remedied immediately because of safety issues.

6. To satisfy Lisa's need for career advancement, she may consider going back to school. She has been working in the library for ten years and has an administrator position. The only real career advancement for her would be librarian. Because she was a teacher at the beginning of her career, she could consider an MLIS degree.

7. If the benefits of Lisa's position outweigh the concerns, Lisa may choose to do nothing. She is happy with her job and enjoys the freedom in the mornings to run errands and because she is a night owl, she enjoys the hours.

Alternative scenarios

Write an analysis of the case study as it is presented or develop an alternative scenario and suggest a possible solution.

Discussion questions

1. What should Lisa do about her frustrations and concerns?

2. What is Lisa's supervisor's responsibility in this situation?

3. How can the library provide opportunities for professional development?

4. Describe a situation when you or a colleague faced a situation like Lisa's. How did you manage this situation? How could you have more effectively managed the situation?

Censorship issues

Sammy Dees

In a small public library in a medium-sized Alabama city, a library director faced a problem concerning the Mel Gibson film *The Passion of the Christ* and its inclusion in the library's holdings.

The 2003 film directed by Mel Gibson, *The Passion of the Christ*, sparked a national debate all over the United States because of its graphic depiction of the last days of Jesus Christ and the views the director had of the Jewish people who were ultimately responsible for Christ's crucifixion. The film is rated R and the library has had a policy that it does not purchase or collect R-rated movies.

Mrs Betty Grayson, director of the Adams Public Library in Adams, Alabama, was presented with a dilemma concerning the inclusion of this film in her medium-sized collection of DVDs that the library stocks. While not a magnet of DVDs that the public can check out, the library's collection nevertheless does provide DVD films for library patrons to check out and view without having to pay heavy rental prices and fines at the local video store.

Mrs Grayson, who was cognizant of the film's content as well as its reputation, went to the local multiplex and viewed the film. At that particular point she decided that, while the film was true to her beliefs and was a well-made production, she would not buy the film on DVD for the library when it was released.

As time went by and the film's box office and headlines grew, the library began to receive requests for *The Passsion of the Christ* DVD. Mrs Grayson decided to take the situation to the Library Board for recommendation since the library's policy did not allow R-rated movies to be stocked in the library's collection. On taking it to the Board, the majority of whom had seen the movie at the theater, she told them of the many requests the library was receiving for copies to be available for check-out. The Board, while recognizing the film's graphic content, decided that despite the R-rating, the content was true to what happened according to biblical teachings, therefore the decision would be Mrs Grayson's and they would support her on the issue.

Other concerned citizens wrote letters to the editor of the local newspaper expressing their disapproval of the movie. The letters indicated that the citizens did not think that video stores should stock the R-rated version, or if they did, they needed to monitor its check-out to adults only and should not rent it to adolescents or children. At the time, the citizens were not aware that the library was contemplating purchasing the DVD for their collection. Soon local TV and newspaper reporters were contacting the library and asking if the library would purchase a copy of the DVD, *The Passion of the Christ*. Mrs Grayson explained her position and informed viewers that the Board had left the decision to her discretion. She explained that while the content was graphic, the film was not exploitative as most R-rated movies are, and that her decision about purchasing the DVD and its check-out procedures would be forthcoming.

As the DVD was released, Mrs Grayson decided to order three copies of the DVD and devised a check-out procedure for this title. She held the copies behind the library desk and would only check out copies to adult library patrons. Patrons requesting this title would have to show identification proving that they were over 18 in order to check out *The Passion of the Christ*. While the controversy of the library having the title was minimal Mrs Grayson's method of letting it be checked out proved successful and the library's circulation of the title was the highest of any other DVD or video title ever made available.

The factors that made this incident interesting were that a management decision on the part of the head of the library, Mrs Grayson, was handled with professionalism and a minimum of negative criticism. She was wise to know the content of the movie before it came to the library, and was experienced enough in her job to take the situation to the Board of Directors of the library *before* the controversy started and got their approval to handle it in the way she saw fit. If she had the Board's support, then the controversy, while present, was small enough that it passed without much interference and general indifference.

Case study analysis

Wendell C. Stone

The issue of violating established policy to add *The Passion of the Christ* to a library's collection presents fascinating challenges, particularly since a sizeable number of the facility's patrons will likely be angered, regardless of the decision. The situation raises significant legal problems, and clearly calls into question the issue of separation of church and state. Much of the decision-making process of the director and the Board of Adams Public Library seems highly subjective and too reliant on religious bias.

One of my concerns has to do with the repercussions of violating an explicit library policy. Operating firmly within policy boundaries provides little enough protection from legal or other action, but at least one has the policy to point to in one's defense. Knowingly violating institutional policy seems to expose the library and the director to unnecessary risks. When a policy no longer serves its purpose, when it no longer acts as an effective guide in decision-making and management, it seems better to change the policy than to ignore it.

As the director, Mrs Grayson should be very concerned about what my vote on the issue means. If the Board has established a policy that Adams Public Library will acquire no movies with a rating of R or higher and if the Board then authorizes the purchase and shelving of a movie with an R rating, has the Board thus implicitly amended its policy? If so, how? What does that mean for future decisions about R-rated movies?

Whether the policy is changed explicitly or implicitly, I am concerned about the reasons for the change and what that says about the new policy. It seems that the new policy is 'Adams Public Library will not circulate R-rated movies unless they present a Christian message that is biblically accurate.' The reasoning of the Board is particularly disturbing: 'The Board, while recognizing the film's graphic content, decided that despite the R-rating, the content was true to what happened according to biblical teachings, therefore the decision would be Mrs Grayson's, and they would support her on the issue . . .' Her bias had already been made clear to us: 'the film was true to her beliefs.' Should we acquire only those items true to our beliefs? What if this had been a movie of similar veracity and artistic merit, but sympathetic to Islam or another religion? The impetus to acquire the film resulted in part from requests from patrons, but very clearly from the case study, the decision was primarily rooted in the religious beliefs of those involved.

I am curious as to the arguments made by those people who ran advertisements asking commercial video outlets to restrict the lending of the tape. Were they concerned by the anti-Semitic overtones many people have identified in the film? Were they concerned about the violence? Did they disagree with the film's interpretation of the historical record? Were their views adequately aired at the Board meeting approving the purchase of the movie?

Ultimately, I am disturbed by the decision to purchase *The Passion of the Christ*. Mrs Grayson should be much more comfortable with the action if a clear policy had been defined and if the decision had emerged solely because of the merits of the movie as a movie, not because of the sectarian religious views embedded within the film. Finally, the board seems to have chosen a rather self-serving and self-vindicating route. Rather than make a definitive decision, they place the decision-making power in the hands of the director. They can take credit for the outcome if it is positive; they can place the blame on Director Grayson if the outcome is negative.

As suggested above, if I were in Mrs Grayson's position and had to make the decision about purchasing *The Passion of the Christ*, I would be reluctant to do so. Whether a public library should make R-rated movies available is clearly controversial, especially in small towns and rural communities. Thus most likely any effort to relax the policy regarding items with mature themes and situations will meet with strong opposition. To feel comfortable with acquiring any such movie, she should want a much clearer definition of library policy, including a reasonable assurance that all viewpoints will be treated equally.

Case study analysis

Chris Sharpe

Case situation

The director of a small public Library, Mrs Betty Grayson, was given the authority by the Library Board to decide whether or not to purchase the DVD of Mel Gibson's *The Passion of the Christ*. The library had received requests to have the DVD available, but because the film was rated R it was against the library policy of not allowing R-rated movies in the library's collection. Mrs Grayson decided to make an exception and purchased three copies. She also instituted a special check-out procedure for *The Passion of the Christ* DVDs by allowing only those that show ID to prove that they are over 18 to check the DVD out.

The problem

The director's decision to make an exception to the R-rated policy set a precedent for future exceptions to be made. Patrons may ask for other R-rated movies in the future; some patrons may feel a film such as *Saving Private Ryan*, despite its violent content, may be a good addition to the library collection. What if several patrons request the library to purchase an R-rated film such as Michael Moore's *Fahrenheit 9/11*, which may not be popular with the majority of the community? The director could be accused of practising censorship by denying the requests of DVDs that may not be politically popular in the library's community.

The decision to only allow patrons over 18 years old to check out the R-rated DVD satisfied people who were concerned about children under 18 years old checking out the DVD, but for a library to restrict access to materials to a certain class of patrons may go against the profession's code of ethics. The American Library Association's code of ethics states, 'We distinguish between our personal convictions and professional duties and do not allow our personal beliefs to interfere with fair representation of the aims of our institutions or the provision of access to their information resources.'[1] By placing the DVDs behind the desk and asking for identification to prove the patron's age, the director may be accused of making policies based on her personal beliefs. Allowing patrons of any age to check out an R-rated movie, however, may upset many parents and result in numerous complaints to the director and the Library Board.

The case study does not state if other R-rated movies had been requested and denied in the past. It is also not known if the Library Board had an opinion on check-out procedures if the director were to purchase the DVDs. The Board stated that it would back the director's decision, but if there were complaints about purchasing the DVDs what would be the procedures and how would the Board respond?

Suggested alternative solutions

1. Buy the DVDs, make an exception to the policy, but allow access to all patrons.

2. Do not buy the DVDs and cite the R-rated policy as the reason.

3. Buy the DVDs, allow access to all, and also end the R-rated policy.

The first alternative solution contains the problem of breaking library policy and the possibility of further R-rated requests. Many in the community may also not like having access to R-rated movies for all patrons.

The second alternative solution may be the easiest for the library because the director could simply state *The Passion of the Christ* DVD is not eligible for purchase due to library policy. But if the library implemented this solution it would be denying a popular request from its patrons.

The third alternative solution would be the best choice in terms of fulfilling the patrons' request to buy the DVD and adhering to library professional ethics by discontinuing the restrictions on buying R-rated films and having access to these films to all patrons. Of course, the library does not have to start adding more R-rated films to the collection, but it would not have to break policy in order to fulfill future R-rated movie requests by patrons.

Decision/action

Mrs Grayson's solution to buy the DVDs, make an exception to library policy, and restrict access by age may have been a popular decision with the community, but it raises problems of censorship, library ethics, and breaking policies. To avoid these problems the director should choose alternative solution 3. Ending the R-rated policy and allowing access to all could upset some in the community, and so if the director follows alternative solution 3 then she needs to make sure she has the backing of the Library Board and explain why the no R-rated policy would create problems for future requests and that restrictions on materials is troubling for a library. If there is much criticism and the library board does not back the director's decision, then the library should maintain the no R-rated movie policy and not make an exception by purchasing *The Passion of the Christ* DVDs.

Alternative scenarios

Write an analysis of the case study as it is presented or develop a scenario and suggest a possible solution. This may be a group activity.

Discussion questions

1. Would this situation have been otherwise if the film were *not* a religious film or if it were rated something different, and did Mrs Grayson do the right thing by allowing the title in the library under the circumstances that it was included?

2. Should Mrs Grayson have listened to the citizens of the town as they are the patrons of the library and their tax money is what funds the library?

3. Should Mrs Grayson have stuck by the library's code of 'no R-rated' films despite the subject matter in this instance?

Note

1. American Library Association, 'Code of Ethics of the American Library Association'. Available online at: *http://www.ala.org/ala/oif/statementspols/codeofethics/ codeethics.htm* (accessed July 2006).

Hiring decisions

Nicol Lewis

Introduction

A library director is faced with a difficult hiring decision. After announcing her selection, one of the candidates has come back to challenge her decision.

The case

Brenda Loudermilk, the newly appointed director of the Troup County Library, was charged with hiring a branch manager for one of her system libraries. Ms Loudermilk wished to elevate the status of the county libraries. The ad for the branch manager position stated that preferably the candidate must have at least three years' experience and a college degree. After posting the position, she narrowed the list of candidates to two current employees.

Ginger Hollingsworth, 23, a librarian assistant, had worked with the Troup County Library system for five years. Ms Hollingsworth had worked with the library since graduating from high school. Outside of periodic training provided by the library system, Ms Hollingsworth did not have a college degree or accredited training.

Sara Levin, 23, a graduate of Emory University with a BA in history, had three years of library experience working part-time in her university's internationally acclaimed and technologically advanced Robert Woodruff Library. Ms Levin had worked for the Troup County Library System for one year.

After screening the candidates thoroughly, Ms Loudermilk found herself in a quandary. Both women interviewed well, had a great work ethic, came with stellar references, and were very adept in library practices. However, after careful consideration, Ms Loudermilk offered the position to Ms Hollingsworth.

Shortly after announcing her decision to the library staff, Ms Levin requested a meeting with Ms Loudermilk to express her discontent with the decision. Ms Levin outlined the reasons why she was a more qualified candidate, which included her having a college degree as well as work experience in a more advanced library system. Ms Levin questioned her future under management that did not value her credentials.

Ms Loudermilk pondered how best to address Ms Levin's concerns.

Case study analysis

Kenneth N. McCullers

This case study presents a situation that some have most certainly faced. Brenda Loudermilk had to hire a branch manager for her system and had narrowed her choice to two candidates that were equally satisfactory in this case. The study tells us that they both did well in interviews, had 'stellar references,' and 'great work ethic[s].' They were also adept at library practices, which I interpret to mean Troup County Library practices.

There are several facts in this case study that should not escape notice. It is stated at the outset that the director herself is newly appointed. Also, she has an interest in 'elevating the status of the county libraries.' The qualifications listed for a branch manager include a minimum of three years of experience and preferably a college degree. The job announcement does not give any information about the job duties or expectations, which should be a part of hiring decisions. It is not clear whether she set the goals for elevating the status of the county libraries herself, or if the library board helped to establish these goals.

In this case, both candidates have the minimum three years of library experience, and only one of the two has a college degree. Ms Levin's previous work experience was in a large college library, and we are told that this was a part-time position. Many questions were unanswered about her experience, especially regarding job responsibilities. It is not clear whether any previous supervisory tasks were a part of her job. She has only had one year of work experience in her current position, if one is considering seniority.

Ms Levin's total work experience does not equal the five years of the chosen candidate, Ms. Hollingsworth. One is tempted to infer from the reading that this candidate's position is full-time, since she has worked there since high school. Also, we might speculate that she has not been concurrently attending college, since the particulars of college-related experience were explicitly stated for Ms Levin. This is not certain, however. It is known that Ms Hollingsworth's work experience has been gained solely with the current employer, Troup County Public Library. One might suppose that she has a broader knowledge of the inner workings of her system, which occurs over time. This experience may have outweighed the value of a college degree in this case, so her education inside the system must carry a particular benefit to the director. We are told that she is a library assistant, and since the job duties for this position are not given, we can only speculate regarding any possible supervisory experience. It is clear that the quality and length of her work experience were final weighing points for Ms Loudermilk.

It seems to me that the main problems to be addressed here are communication and interpersonal relations. Therefore the specific action required by this case study is a carefully conducted conference with an aggrieved employee. Assuming that Ms Loudermilk made her decision based on the factors outlined above, we are not told whether she is uncertain to any degree about her own decision, but this can have a significant impact on the content of her conversation with Ms Levin. One assumes that she wants to retain Ms Levin as an employee given her outstanding qualifications for the position, and reassure Levin of her value to the library. Hopefully, Ms Loudermilk will be able to start the conversation by attempting to put Ms Levin at ease, just as in the interview process. If the interviews were conducted with a standard set of questions as recommended by Stueart and Moran (2002), the director can also reassure Levin of the fairness of the interview process, especially if this is mandated by county policy.

Perhaps there are other factors to consider as well, such as the current goals of the system and the pace at which it can reach those goals. If Levin has the perspective of a 'more advanced' system (although this qualification itself in a public vs. academic context is a questionable value judgement), this may well be useful in upcoming days when the system continues its growth.

Perhaps there are other personality issues given in Ms Loudermilk's choice that she can address carefully. Does Ms Levin's view of the superiority of her degree and college work experience as an interview candidate also factor into her relations with others on a day-to-day basis, or is this simply part of her defense of her qualifications? Does her reaction to question her value 'under management who didn't value such credentials' imply unhappiness with current administration or policies, or is she simply making a snap judgement regarding her future based on this experience? If the less flattering view of Ms Levin's motivations is correct, then a carefully thought out response could have the value of redirecting Ms Levin toward better work habits and a future promotion. Perhaps the less flattering view is not correct, and Ms Loudermilk already has other long-term opportunities in mind for Ms Levin instead of this one. This is yet another assumption, but offers a much more positive direction in reassuring Ms Levin if indeed it is the case.

It is clear that in trying to assuage and motivate Ms Levin as an employee, the director must approach this conversation with great care. Both candidates are young and much less experienced than she. Hopefully, maturity and wisdom will allow her to gracefully address these difficult issues.

Alternative scenarios

1. Select one of the alternative scenarios below and describe how you would deal with this additional information if you were Ms Levin.

(a) A newspaper reporter comes in to interview Ms Hollingsworth about her new job. She sees Sara Levin working at the circulation desk and stops to chat with her. The newspaper reporter is on the library board and was a friend of Sara Levin's while she was at Emory. The newspaper reporter said, 'Sara, I sure am sorry that you did not get the job. I think everyone on the board was afraid that with a new baby you would need to be out a lot or may decide to quit work.'

(b) Ms Loudermilk discloses to Sara Levin that the board has voted to open a new branch in July. She thought it best to go ahead and appoint Ms Hollingsworth as branch manager so that Ms Levin could continue to work with her at the main branch until the new branch opens. However, a few days later, Sara overhears Ms Loudermilk talking with a friend. 'You will not believe what I have been through with this know-it-all that came to us from Emory. She got all huffy about not being appointed branch manager. I mentioned the new branch to try to appease her but you had better believe I'm going to do everything I can to see to it that they do not appoint her to this position. She is nothing but trouble.'

2. Discuss the list of criteria that Ms Loudermilk should have used to make a fair, defensible decision.

Reference

Stueart, R. and Moran, B. (2002) *Library and Information Center Management*, 6th edn. Greenwood Village, CO: Libraries Unlimited.

To terminate or not to terminate, that is the question

Matthew Sunrich

Introduction

A new extension librarian is not adequately performing her duties. She has allegedly made inappropriate sexual advances to staff members. Her supervisor has talked with her and must decide what disciplinary action should be taken.

The case

Responding to an ad, Maria came to West Central Technical College (WCTC) seeking a position as librarian. She had previously been a librarian at the Southern University, which seemed like a good sign. During the interviewing process, Janet, the library director, was pleased with her. It was unclear why Maria had left her position at Southern University, but she had received a positive recommendation from her previous employer, so Janet didn't feel it necessary to press the issue. Maria had an accredited MLS, a professional demeanor, and seemed like a good candidate. Janet offered her the job.

At this time, the growing WCTC was in the process of

adding a second branch library. Janet had been with the system for almost ten years, and she had been appointed branch manager at the new branch. The only other librarian, Dan, worked at the other branch. Janet and Dan had to finagle their schedules to cover the lunch schedules because of the limited staff. Hiring Maria was going to make things a lot easier, although they would still be understaffed, or, as Janet put it, 'stretched thin.' There were two full-time library assistants and a handful of student workers, but operating two libraries (with a third one to come) often demanded more than the staff could handle.

Maria got off to a bad start when she showed up with her children in tow for her first day of work. She had somehow gotten the idea that daycare would be provided. Janet explained that this was not the case and gave Maria a week to make daycare arrangements for her children before returning to work. Maria apologized and explained that she was going through a divorce. This seemed plausible enough, but in time it would become rather difficult to tell when Maria was telling the truth about anything.

While the new library was being completed, Maria worked with Janet. Things seemed all right at first. Maria wasn't a particularly hardworking employee, but she did what was expected of her. It seemed to Janet that Maria was one of those people who were content to do the bare minimum and not to take the initiative. While this was certainly not an admirable characteristic, Janet did not expect it to present a problem. After all, there are a great many people in the workforce who share this ethic.

When the new library opened, Janet assigned Maria to manage the central library. Maria had the credentials and the experience, so Janet trusted her in this capacity. Almost immediately, things at Maria's library began to go downhill. During her visits to the library, it became emphatically clear to Janet that Maria was not doing any work. When confronted, Maria made all kinds of excuses. Maria insisted that she was unable to get the work done due to being understaffed, which could certainly account for some of the problems, but the most basic necessities, such as circulation desk coverage, were not being achieved.

The patrons were not even receiving the minimum level of service. Serials were not being checked in, there were serious issues with the reception and allocation of the mail, morale among her student workers was low because there was no clear indication of management, and necessary policies and procedures were not being followed, which was particularly bad because neglecting to follow policies directly affected the other libraries. The other libraries had to constantly address issues and problems relating to the lack of consistency and carelessness at Maria's branch.

Maria had a lot of personal issues outside of work that were interfering with her job. At one point she claimed that her father had passed away and at another that she had developed breast cancer. Based on Maria's previous mendacity, Janet did not know whether either of these things or anything else she said was true.

As if all of this weren't bad enough, Maria had a peculiar personality that even the staff outside of the library found distressing. She was, by all accounts, downright strange. Some people were even afraid of her. Even more bizarrely, it later came out that she was making sexual advances toward some of the maintenance staff.

Janet had numerous discussions with her, but there were no apparent changes in her behavior. The simple answer would have been, obviously, to terminate her, but Janet was in a tough position because if she were to fire Maria the libraries would have a real mess on their hands. If it had been hard enough to manage two libraries with insufficient staff, managing three would have been an impossible task. Had Maria been a part-time employee, it would have been much easier to get rid of her, but her full-time, professional status designated her as an important part of the system, even if the quality of her work was appalling.

Fortunately, Maria decided to leave of her own volition. Janet was able to find a new librarian to fill Maria's position fairly quickly.

Case study analysis

Tara McCann

I have selected Matthew Sunrich's case study for analysis and am using the Northeastern University Cases Analysis Model listed as a web resource on our syllabus.

The situation

The personnel problem presented is a common scenario in many businesses today: inadequately prepared staff put in managerial/human resource roles who are somehow expected to make very serious personnel decisions on the spot with little training, experience, or education in the acquisition and maintenance of human resources. Janet, like many library directors, was placed in this role armed with a generic MLIS and on-the-job training while heading up multiple academic library branches. Unfortunately for Janet, when a seemingly good candidate for the job applied Janet assumed that Maria would be a perfect fit. But because of Maria's lack of work ethic and questionable mental stability, Janet wasted time, effort, and library resources on a damaging personnel problem. Ideally, proper management training would have armed Janet with the tools she needed to manage a difficult staff member like Maria.

The facts

A listing of the known facts is as follows:

1. Janet was given the task of hiring a new librarian.
2. There was a time constraint to have the librarian hired and in place before the new library opened.
3. Maria failed to run the library as Janet expected.
4. Janet felt she couldn't fire Maria because there was no one to take her place.

Identify the problems/causes

Janet was given a human resources job which she was ill-equipped to handle effectively – I equate it with a teacher rising to the position of school principal with no other degree or training than a teacher's certificate. Janet was essentially doing the job of three people: the director, the librarian, and the human resource manager; in fact, it is entirely possible that with only one other professional librarian on staff (Dan) Janet may or may not have been involved in the hiring process at all. On top of all these job responsibilities Janet was in the throes of hatching a new library, so of course she didn't have the time to put Maria through a thorough hiring process as a human resource manager would do if that were one of her main responsibilities.

Secondly, there must have been some misunderstanding about the position. There was no job description other than 'Librarian' and if Maria felt childcare was provided then perhaps Janet spent more time selling the position than outlining it. A job description is an essential tool for avoiding misunderstandings. Even if there was a job description, how could Janet effectively train/guide Maria into the standard operating procedures and policies of the library when Janet had to be immediately present at the new branch at all times? Every library is different and it takes an average of several weeks before most employees feel they have the procedures 'down' enough to be confident in job execution.

Maria was probably not prepared to go from librarian to a director of her own branch, and obviously did not have the familial resources or stability to devote to such a task. Although Maria came as an 'experienced' and 'recommended' librarian, managing an entire unfamiliar library is a daunting task for any aspiring director, let alone a regular librarian. If Maria had no such aspirations, then the jobs of scheduling an entire staff and managing all aspects and menial tasks of a library would certainly be overwhelming, even for an enthusiastic librarian with a great work ethic. Maria appears to have just needed a job.

Alternative solutions and plan

Janet was wearing too many hats to be an effective leader and supervisor. She should have clamored for more personnel to take on some of her job responsibilities or for human resources at the college to perform some of the preliminary background/reference checks. Janet was being too optimistic in fitting Maria into the job description; Janet is in desperate need of some management courses or human resource allocation/management classes which are probably offered at no cost for her right there through West Central Technical College. Janet could have armed herself with the knowledge (and the paperwork) to point to Maria's failings and put her on probation or suspension to improve her behavior. Janet should also have had several good candidates to interview for this position before settling on Maria and having several names to call in a pinch would have bolstered her enough to reprimand Maria and temper the desperateness Janet felt in the situation. Also, having a generic written recommendation is different to taking the time and effort to call several references and inquire about Maria's ability to direct and manage an entire library and staff. Janet was doing too many jobs to do one thoroughly or well.

Maria trespassed on Janet's good faith and trust, so of course some blame does lie with her. However, her havoc in the libraries would have been lessened if Janet had the tools and resources to deal with a difficult staff member like Maria. Very few professions would have tolerated Maria's behavior so it was a shame that she could not have learned this lesson months earlier and at the college's expense, too. Janet should specify that the next candidate must have management classes and experience. Maria could have taken business or management classes at the college for no cost, so perhaps this option could be offered to the next candidate.

Alternative scenarios

1. Write an analysis of the case study as it is presented or develop a scenario and suggest a possible solution. You may work in pairs or as a group.

2. Janet turned on the evening news. The news anchor announced, 'A West Central Technical College librarian is being held in the county jail tonight on charges of statutory rape. Ms Maria Martin of the West Central Technical College branch library was arrested this

afternoon following a lead from an unidentified 14-year-old boy who confessed to his grandmother that Ms Martin was pregnant and that he was the father of her child. The teen reported that Ms Martin had seduced numerous teens who had gone to the library for the after-school tutoring program.'

Janet went to the library the next morning to open the library. She did not expect to have an encounter with Maria. Maria's mother had posted bail for her and Maria was unlocking the door just as Janet arrived. 'I guess you saw the news last night?' Maria questioned. Maria continued before Janet had a chance to respond. 'Can you believe people make up stuff like that? I'll have to get a lawyer but I am going to prove that kid is lying. It is true that I am pregnant but my ex-husband is the father.' What course of action should Janet follow?

3. Janet has heard rumors that Maria is involved with drugs. She drove past her house one evening and noticed that the windows had all been painted black. Several of the patrons had recently complained about the increase in the price of fines and library services at the branch where Maria worked. Janet had tried several times to contact Maria to confirm her questions about these new charges and increased fines. Maria had failed to return her calls. Janet noticed that Maria's monthly financial report did not indicate an increase in funds. Janet apprised Dan of her suspicions. The next day Dan came in with some distressing news. 'Janet, I just got a call from the police station. A freshman at West Central Technical College was taken to the emergency room last night. She had overdosed on methamphetamines. They asked her where she got the drugs and she said that she and some other students had purchased the meth from Maria Martin.'

Discussion questions

1. Had Maria not left, though, what course of action should Janet have taken to resolve the problem?

2. What guidelines might Janet adopt in the future when screening candidates for employment?

Privacy issues

Haley Mims and Leah Dasher

Introduction

Cindy, a paraprofessional, works at a public library's circulation desk. While helping a patron one day, Cindy inquired about the patron's interest in adoption. Lynn, the patron, felt uneasy with this inquiry and left. Then Cindy mentioned Lynn's interest in adoption to a mutual friend. Lynn was irate when she learned that Cindy had divulged this private information and called the director demanding that Cindy be fired.

Case study

Cindy is a 22-year-old who works as a paraprofessional at the City Library's circulation desk. Her director encourages all of the staff to get to know their patrons. The director said that is one of the best ways to exhibit good customer service is by showing patrons that the staff are interested not only in the books they read, but in their hobbies, their families, and their jobs.

Cindy has always been a popular young lady with a

fun-loving personality and Cindy enjoys asking questions and getting to know the patrons on a personal level.

One day Lynn, a regular library patron, asked Cindy to help her locate some books on adoption. Cindy took that as an opening to ask questions about Lynn's interest in adoption. She asked her how long she had been trying to have a child and if she had considered fertility treatments or surrogacy. Lynn did not want to go into the details of her private struggle with infertility, so she told Cindy she would just find the books herself. Cindy was oblivious to the woman's look of irritation and followed her to the shelves where the adoption books were located. She then started telling Lynn about how she thought Angelina Jolie was so wonderful to have adopted those third-world country children and asked if that was what Lynn wanted to do.

Lynn was used to answering questions from friends and family about her infertility, but she was taken aback by Cindy's barrage of questions. Not one to usually speak her mind, Lynn quietly told Cindy she just remembered that she had to be somewhere and quickly left.

Although the library was fairly small, none of the other staff had overheard the conversation nor seen Lynn leave.

One day Cindy was talking with her friend Katie who was also considering adoption, and she remembered Lynn's recent visit to the library. She told Katie about Lynn's interest in adoption, and Katie said she knew Lynn from church. Cindy suggested that Katie call Lynn so they could discuss their similar situations and perhaps offer advice and encouragement to one another.

The next day, the library director received a phone call from Lynn who was very upset. She told the director how Cindy had embarrassed her when she was in the library and how she had also told other people about her interest in adoption. She told the director that at the doctor's office where she worked she would have been fired for asking a patient such personal questions and especially for revealing private information about a patient to someone else.

The director assured Lynn that she would address her concerns with Cindy, but Lynn was adamant that Cindy should be fired.

Discussion questions

1. Is it appropriate for the director to encourage the employees to 'get to know the patrons better'?

2. What action should the director take?

3. What new policies should possibly come from this situation?

A question of service:
a case study of a
bookmobile incident

Tara McCann

Introduction

A bookmobile librarian turns personal problems and her political agenda into an agenda for the library. She purchases books and plans activities around her political agenda. Another bookmobile librarian is caught in the dilemma of whether to defend her colleague or to listen sympathetically to patrons who do not agree with her colleague.

The case

In a Midwestern university town, a district library relied heavily on its bookmobile service to bring books and material to local schools that no longer had school libraries due to drastic funding cuts. The bookmobile also served 3–4 assisted living facilities for the elderly, a government subsidized house project, and outlying suburbs and neighborhoods with no library branches nearby due to recent city sprawl.

The woman who managed the bookmobile was a recent university graduate named Candice. Candice had a BA in history and was accepted into an MLIS program at a nearby university. Candice kept deferring her enrollment due to undergraduate bills. She had agreed to obtain her MLIS within five years when she was hired as the bookmobile librarian.

The bookmobile was considered to be a separate branch of its own with its own budget and Candice was to perform collection development, weeding, stock rotation, the acquiring of educational material aids, and cataloging. There were managers of circulation and reference at the main branch, and Candice reported directly to the library director, Ms 'M.' Ms M kept her door closed when she was in her office and relied on one-way communication through memos to direct staff and keep them updated on policies she changed or enacted.

When Candice's part-time college student assistant gave notice that she was moving away from the area, a young married woman named Teresa was hired for the position by the director. Teresa was to come in to the western branch every afternoon during the week and help Candice load books and materials from her office into the bookmobile, assist patrons, and then help Candice unload the materials and download the laptop into the mainframe computer.

The two women got along well and Candice was soon relying a lot on Teresa. Candice took the time to train Teresa and explained why she took certain materials on certain days, based on the stops for that day's schedule, like an elementary school, middle school, or an assisted living facility. Candice was very organized with one wall of her office covered with built-in shelves all carefully labeled for each day and for each stop – books requested by patrons or books that might be requested based on upcoming holidays or events. When Candice became pregnant, Teresa expressed her desire for the bookmobile not to miss any stops or days. Candice felt confident to leave the bookmobile to Teresa when she had to be away for prenatal visits and various appointments. Teresa noticed the small adult non-fiction section on the bookmobile growing even though they had a small adult clientele. Most seniors gave Candice lists of favorite authors or books and the two women delivered these requests right to the seniors' doors in the living center. Candice spent a lot of time reading and ordering baby name and pregnancy books with the justification that teens may be looking for these books. When Candice started having problems with her boyfriend, 'relationship' books were purchased.

Candice seemed to change almost overnight into a surly, angry person and even her politics took a hard swing left. As they were in an election year, Candice invested bookmobile money on the published works of a certain political party and expressed hostility toward books that promoted family values or traditions. As Thanksgiving neared, Candice pulled all the Christmas books off the bookmobile and replaced them with alternative holiday books – with multiple copies of the same titles. Candice also became outspoken with patrons about her political beliefs and criticized traditional family values, sometimes to parents with kids in tow. Teresa was admittedly glad when Candice took three months of maternity leave before Christmas and immediately restocked the bookmobile with Christmas books because Christmas books were requested at every stop. Since Teresa was temporarily working full-time, she traveled to the branches to collect material and learned that patrons were complaining about Candice's behavior and outspoken political views. Teresa was a non-confrontational person so she busied herself with filling the needs and requests of the bookmobile.

When Candice came back from maternity leave, she was understandably unhappy about leaving her baby. Teresa was a mother too and tried to be supportive, but Candice was resentful that Teresa's husband was watching their child while Candice had to put her baby in daycare. Candice developed a schedule for pumping breast milk but this required a mid-afternoon run back to the hosting branch to store the delicate milk, which cut one entire stop out of their run every day. Teresa felt bad for Candice so she remained flexible and supportive, unaware if the director even knew of the interrupted bookmobile schedule. Candice sometimes cancelled bookmobile schedules if she decided to call in sick at the last moment, which didn't give Teresa enough time to gather material to do the run by herself. Frustrated, Teresa applied to library school and picked up extra hours at the other branches. She heard co-workers complain about Candice's erratic and hostile behavior but tried not to comment because she felt Candice was more like a friend than a co-worker.

Candice began to order multiple copies of alternative sexuality and specialty books like *Heather Has Two Mommies* and *Daddy's Roommate* and even children's chapter books about girls falling in love with their girlfriends and boys expressing their sexuality to other boys. Teresa noticed the adult non-fiction section growing again with 'coming out' books and agreed that these books should be in the library system but that they didn't seem to be relevant to the particular patrons the bookmobile served. When Teresa questioned Candice about the application of the books, Candice justified that if one mixed-up kid finds 'enlightenment' out of just one book, she will be doing her job. Teresa didn't agree with the bookmobile becoming Candice's 'agenda machine' but didn't know the path of authority and had only met the director once when she was hired.

One snowy night, as Teresa was finishing the bookmobile run by herself because Candice called in sick, a parent lingered to complain to Teresa about what she felt were 'inappropriate and morally reprehensible picture books' in the collection. Teresa tried to explain that the library had to offer a variety of material to a varied demographic, but the parent insisted the bookmobile had a set, particular demographic and that if anyone wanted these books, they could go to the main, downtown branch and get them. Teresa could only shrug and agree with the hostile parent, and suggested the parent call the director of the library system in the morning and express her views.

The next day, Teresa was called into the director's office and was told she acted unprofessionally and intolerantly when she failed to support a co-worker in front of a patron. Ms 'M' was furious that Teresa breached confidence by voicing agreement with this patron. Ms 'M' accused Teresa of being a narrow-minded, religious bigot and immediately dismissed her from the bookmobile. Teresa was offered a position at the circulation desk if she promised that no more derisive behavior would occur. She was told that a copy of the disciplinary action would be put in Teresa's evaluation file. Teresa was devastated, as the director promised never to recommend her for a job or give her a recommendation letter for library school. Teresa left the public library system and became a teacher. Candice was not terminated for never attaining her MLIS and fellow library workers grumbled that firing a single lesbian mother would be 'a bad political move' in a university town.

Case study analysis

Matthew Sunrich

Comprehend the case situation: collect data, identify relevant facts

Teresa, a young married woman, takes a part-time position as an assistant to Candice, the bookmobile manager. Teresa is responsible for loading materials onto the bookmobile, going on runs, assisting patrons, and performing basic computer operations. Several school libraries have been forced to shut down due to budget constraints, and there are a number of senior citizens, lower-income families, and residents of outlying subdivisions who cannot make it to the library. Teresa takes pride in the bookmobile's ability to provide service to these patrons, and she wants nothing more than to satisfy the community. Because the bookmobile always serves the same patrons, Teresa and Candice are familiar with the sorts of titles that the bookmobile should carry in order to satisfy patron needs and reading interests.

Define the problem

Candice and Teresa get along very well until Candice begins to use bookmobile funds to purchase books for herself, although she denies that this is the case. Although the books Candice adds to the collection initially deal with pregnancy and resolving relationships problems (issues that she is facing), Teresa soon finds that Candice is stocking the bookmobile with materials that promote the politics to which she subscribes and is removing books that oppose her political views. As the holidays approach, Candice pulls all of the Christmas-themed books, despite the fact that a demand for these books exists. She becomes very outspoken about her beliefs and critical of others, much to the chagrin of many patrons.

When Candice returns from maternity leave, she complains about having to put her infant in daycare. Her motherly responsibilities begin to interfere with the bookmobile's operations. Candice continues to stock the bookmobile with controversial materials, including children's books dealing with alternative lifestyles, books that are not relevant to the patrons the bookmobile serves. Whenever Teresa confronts Candice about these materials, Candice always finds excuses that seem altruistic. One night, when Teresa is conducting the bookmobile run alone, an angry parent complains that she does not feel that many of the books are appropriate. Teresa attempts to placate her, expresses agreement, and suggests that the patron contact the library director about her concerns.

The next day, Teresa is called into the director's office and is reprimanded for taking the patron's side. The director accuses Teresa of being a religious fanatic and a bigot and relieves her of her position on the bookmobile. Moreover, she is told that she will never receive a professional recommendation. Candice is never terminated, despite that fact that she fails to fulfill the requirement of completing her MLIS within five years. Co-workers attribute this to the fact that she is a lesbian single mother.

Assessment

This is certainly a touchy situation because it involves two controversial political issues, i.e. single motherhood and lesbianism. While it is true that one of the primary responsibilities of libraries is to provide materials on all topics, it is important to remember that some materials are considered inappropriate by some patrons. Almost everything has the potential to be offensive; it is the librarian's job to consider the demographics, patron requests, and circulation patterns and to stock books accordingly. It seems to me that Candice is in the wrong for three reasons:

1. She is purchasing books for herself, which is not what librarians are supposed to do.
2. She is using the bookmobile as a means to further her political agenda.
3. She is not considering the needs of her patrons.

I believe, however, that the library director is just as much at fault as Candice. It seems to me that the library director is behaving in a cowardly fashion. Based on the director's accusations, we can assume that the director sides with Candice, but we cannot know whether she is doing it because of personal convictions or because of societal pressures. Regardless of whether Teresa's handling of the encounter with the angry patron was right or not, the director, in my estimation, overreacted.

Candice uses her sexual orientation and status as a single mother to her advantage. She is aware that she can use both to her political advantage if disciplinary action is taken against her. She feels bulletproof. The library director is right to defend Candice's lifestyle choices, but she is wrong to allow herself to be manipulated by them. A person's lifestyle choices do not make them exempt from disciplinary action. Candice has allowed her personal life to interfere with the operations of the bookmobile and is not satisfying her patrons. She should be reprimanded for these offenses.

The director accuses Teresa of being a religious bigot, but this does not appear to be the case. First of all, conservative views are not intrinsically religious. Morality, regardless of how it is defined, is just as much a societal issue as it is a religious one. To designate conservatism as religious is a knee-jerk reaction. It does not seem to me that Teresa ever brings up religion at all. In fact, the case study specifically states that Teresa is 'non-confrontational.' Teresa is merely attempting to make her patrons happy. Whether or not she agrees with them is irrelevant. She has no agenda, quite unlike Candice. The right thing to do would be to stock the bookmobile with materials that address controversial issues from both points of view. This is a primary concern among acquisitions librarians. They must represent equally both sides of an issue so that no one can accuse the library of being biased.

Perhaps Teresa should not have 'sided' with the angry parent. This is really the only thing that she conceivably did wrong. The director should have told Candice that she could not use the bookmobile as a tool of her political inclinations. If she feels that it is necessary for the bookmobile to carry books that oppose family values, then it needs to carry books that promote them, as well. She should not confront patrons with her political views because this is not appropriate. Her concern should be to provide patrons with the materials they want and leave it at that. It is not the librarian's job to promote or to oppose anything, only to provide requested information.

Case study analysis

Tonda Morris

In this scenario, a community bookmobile operated as a separate library branch. The case was told from a library assistant's point of view. The bookmobile served a suburban area without school libraries. It also served four elderly public housing project areas.

Candice, the manager of the bookmobile, was hired with the understanding that she would obtain an MLIS degree within five years. Teresa was hired as a part-time library assistant for the bookmobile. Candice's pregnancy seemed to coincide with a shift in her personality and work ethics. Candice reportedly became temperamental at work, and her collection development purchases seemed to reflect personal interests. When Candice returned from maternity leave, these behaviors continued. Additionally, Candice cut into the bookmobile's operating schedule to accommodate personal time to deliver breast milk for her new baby.

Over time, patrons began to complain about alternative lifestyle materials in the bookmobile. Teresa sided with a patron in a discussion of the controversial materials and suggested the patron contact the system's library director to complain. The director had a meeting with Teresa the following day, admonishing her for siding with a patron in a discussion regarding another employee. Teresa's position with the bookmobile was terminated. However, she was offered a demotion as a circulation clerk at the main branch with the stipulation that she would never receive a favorable work recommendation. These terms were unacceptable to Teresa so she resigned. Candice continued as the bookmobile manager without being required to obtain an MLIS degree.

Teresa appeared to be a conscientious and dedicated employee. She was in a difficult situation as her employment issues involved a supervisor as opposed to a co-worker. Unfortunately, a lack of involvement or support from the library administration resulted in her not having knowledge of or access to professional guidance when confronting such complicated and sensitive work issues.

Identification of issues

- *Contract breech*
    - Candice did not fulfill her employment contract. She never enrolled in an MLIS program and therefore never fulfilled the educational requirements of her employment contract.
    - The library administration never addressed this breech.

- *Discrimination*
    - Library employees seemed to take issue with Candice's personal lifestyle choices.

- *Censorship*
    - Reportedly, some of Candice's collection development purchases were personally biased.
    - Patrons wanted to determine what materials could and could not be in the bookmobile collection.
    - Teresa publicly took a personal stand on material selection by agreeing with a patron.

- *Management*
    - Management did not enforce employee contract stipulations.
    - The bookmobile was operating without supervision by management.
    - A chain of command between employees and management was not apparent.
    - The library director acted on an employee issue without investigating the entire situation.

Alternative solutions

- *Contract breech*
  - The library administration should have enforced Candice's contract agreement in regard to her obtaining an MLIS degree in the five-year specified time-frame. If this was personally difficult for Candice to accomplish due to her personal situation, she could have attempted to renegotiate her contract with an extended time-frame for obtaining the degree.
  - When Candice refused to pursue her promised educational aspirations, she should have been demoted to another position in the library system in which an MLIS degree was not required.

- *Discrimination*
  - The fact that Candice's lesbianism surfaced is in itself indicative of discrimination. Professional collection development procedures could have been discussed with Candice without referring to her personal lifestyle.
  - It is not professional for employees to judge their co-workers' personal lifestyle choices. It is unethical for a librarian to discuss a fellow employee's job performance or personal lifestyle with a patron.

- *Censorship*
  - Teresa should have followed a chain of command in trying to inform the library administration of her concerns about the bookmobile's collection development. She should have followed the same procedure for reporting difficulties with her supervisor and for patron complaints.
  - Teresa should have been more aggressive in seeking support from the library director. Perhaps she would have received support and/or suggestions for

interacting appropriately with Candice and for addressing patron complaints professionally.

- *Poor management*
  - By not enforcing Candice's contract stipulation regarding education, Candice did not have the knowledge to operate the bookmobile according to professional guidelines and ethics. If she had entered an MLIS program, she would have been in a position to acquire knowledge and expertise needed to manage the bookmobile in a professional and ethical manner.
  - Management should have monitored the bookmobile operation.
  - A chain of command should have been established between employees and management.
  - Investigating the entire situation regarding the patron complaint would have given the library director a more complete picture of the situation. This might have resulted in retaining a dedicated employee who was willing to seek an MLIS degree. It would also have illuminated the need for administrative involvement in the bookmobile's management.

Recommended implementation strategies

Reportedly, Teresa never directly confronted Candice about their conflicts or the patron complaints. If she had approached Candice when the issues first arose, perhaps they could have worked out an appropriate, professional solution. If talking to Candice proved ineffectual, documentation of the bookmobile issues Teresa confronted would have been her best line of defense. She could have taken her documentation to the library director as the various events unfolded.

The library director's admonishment of Teresa seemed harsh. While Teresa was wrong in expressing her personal opinion to a patron, it sounds like she had never previously been reprimanded for her job performance. Apparently until the patron incident, the library director did not know about the ongoing bookmobile operational and personnel problems. The library director should have asked to hear Teresa's account of the incident and considered her viewpoint and actions with this information in mind before making administrative decisions.

Management should always hear both sides of a controversy involving employees. The bookmobile was being operated as a branch library without a qualified librarian in charge. The two bookmobile employees were seemingly unsupervised. If the director changed her mind about requiring Candice to get a library degree, she should have required Candice to attend workshops or courses to obtain more professional expertise in operating a branch library as well as in supervising an employee.

Follow-up

The most effective strategy the library director could have employed regarding the bookmobile's operation would have been to establish regular staff meetings with the bookmobile employees. This type of management involvement would have ensured the library's policies and procedures were being adhered to and given the library director a way to document personnel requirements and recommendations. Staff meetings would have provided a communication channel for all involved to express their thoughts, concerns, and feelings regarding any bookmobile or employment issues. It also would have allowed management to stay abreast of all aspects of the bookmobile's part in the operation of the library system.

Candice and Teresa seemed to work well together the majority of the time and both seemed to have many of the skills and abilities needed in their respective positions. Open communication between them may have prevented the ensuing chain of events and perhaps would have resulted in a more effective and satisfying work environment for both of the bookmobile employees.

Alternative scenarios

Write an analysis of the case study as it is presented or develop a scenario and suggest a possible solution. This can be a group activity.

Discussion questions

1. How should Teresa have acted in a more professionally responsible manner?

2. When the patron called the library director to complain about the materials on the bookmobile, the library director recognized that the library policy manual was in serious need of being updated. Suggest wording for policies that would address the issues that are involved in this case. Refer to appropriate American Library Association policies in developing your policies.

3. When the patron called the library director about the materials on the bookmobile, the library director contacted the members of the library board. What points should they consider when making their decision about whether or not to terminate Teresa?

Here's the new library, where are the staff?

Maradith H. Sheffield

Introduction

A new college library has purchased new furniture, automation software, computers, books, and materials. The librarian is also maintaining a full-time teaching load. She is concerned because the library will officially open next fall and no plans have been made to make her position in the library full-time or to hire any other staff members.

The case

The new college library is in year two of its initial startup. So far the library has an automation system in place, furniture, student computer workstations, periodicals, and a limited number of books on the shelves. The work thus far has been completed by the acting librarian.

When the acting librarian began employment at the school, her given job title was Program Chair of one of the departments and Instructor for that department. Over the course of her two years at the school, she has been a Program Chair and has taught full-time in addition to her library duties.

During the 2005–2006 fiscal year, she began work on the library at the school. The library now has a functioning automation system, furniture, student computer workstations, periodicals, and a limited number of books on the shelves. The library also has all of the reference books previously housed in each department at the school. However, most of the resources are not yet cataloged. All of this work was completed sporadically over the course of this past year.

The sporadic work schedule in the library is due to the acting librarian's schedule within the department she chairs and as a full-time instructor. Over the past year, she has conducted the recruiting, managing, and student advisement for her department. She has been responsible for teaching classes within her department as well as business and English courses within other departments throughout the school. The acting librarian has also begun to teach a couple of academic courses that are required in all program areas. She has averaged about five courses per quarter over the past year. This meant that she was in the classroom a minimum of five hours a day. Some of the classes were online; however, online classes still require basically the same amount of time each day. Also, time was spent daily answering student questions and grading student work. At the end of 40 hours each week, there was still plenty left to be done within her IT department, at committee meetings, and in other instructor duties. The library duties, many weeks, were left undone.

This coming year is slated to be the year that the library is completed. This will consist of cataloging all the resources already collected by the library from the different departments throughout the school, ordering and cataloging new resources, and cataloging and storing the periodicals already being received by the library. Besides acquiring and cataloging resources, patrons need to be added into the cataloging system and the system needs to be tested for any circulation problems. The library also needs to be open during the day to allow students to come in and browse and to utilize library resources. At this time the library is only open a few hours a day. The few hours that the library has been open during past quarters is the time when the librarian is in her office grading papers, returning phone calls, and answering e-mail. She never has time for professional library duties such as cataloging and organizing materials, planning or providing reference services, or marketing the new collection.

It will not be possible for one person to achieve all the goals of year two alone. Another worker is needed in the library. A student has been considered for the job. She will need to volunteer at least 20 hours per week to be able to continue enrollment in a financial aid program. The program allows her to go to school and pays for her childcare. This student is highly competent, hardworking, and trustworthy. The librarian will feel comfortable with training her and leaving her in the library when she is in class. However, she will only be volunteering for one quarter. The amount of work that needs to be done will not be completed in the short ten-week period. Another solution is needed.

Alternative scenarios

Write an analysis of the case study as it is presented or develop a scenario and suggest a possible solution. This can be a group activity.

Discussion questions

1. How should this librarian approach her administration about the need for additional staffing? Consider options such as benchmarking and temporary staffing.

2. Should the librarian have taken on all of these additional responsibilities if they were not listed in her job description?

3. What professional standards would relate to this case?

Can you teach an old dog new tricks?

Kenneth N. McCullers

Introduction

Bonnie loves her job at the Piccadilly Branch Library until computers invade her territory. The library manager is faced with a difficult dilemma when he insists Bonnie use the new automated system. She sets out to prove the old adage, 'You can't teach an old dog new tricks.'

The case

Bonnie has been working at the Piccadilly Branch Library of the Sommerville Public Library System for a little more than a decade. When Bonnie's husband died later in her life, a friend who worked at the branch encouraged her to apply when a position opened. Bonnie was delighted; she had loved being a Piccadilly Library patron, and now being able to work with her best friend Sue was an added bonus.

Bonnie loved her work at the branch. After an initial period of discomfort learning to work the text-based circulation system, she settled in and began to enjoy her job, especially recommending great books for her friends. There was some staff turnover, but Bonnie loved the new folks, and got along well with her various managers.

The Sommerville system soon saw new growth, and Bonnie saw her branch change from a neighborhood library with a general focus into a branch library focused on children's services. Suddenly, there was more programming for the little people, and the collection changed as well, with more juvenile materials replacing adult materials. Some of Bonnie's friends began to visit less frequently. The library purchased several new computers to meet patron requests for Internet access. Computer problems abounded. Bonnie was barely computer literate. She continually depended on the kindness of a co-worker, to whom she fielded all computer problems.

The worst was yet to come. The Sommerville Library circulation system was upgraded to a new web-based product, and suddenly Bonnie didn't know how to do anything! She was terrified of punching the wrong button and making the computer crash. She took a training class to learn the new system but found it hard to retain what she learned. Bonnie had trouble following lists of written instructions she received in her circulation training packet. She wasn't worried, though, because the Sommerville library system gave everyone a few months to learn the ropes in practice mode before going live. She assumed she would somehow absorb what she needed before the day arrived.

The months flew by. Bonnie's manager repeatedly offered quiet practice time at an office computer away from the circulation desk. Bonnie had trouble concentrating, and always made excuses saying she preferred to practise at a circulation terminal since the software was available there. Bonnie's co-workers took time to practise, but Bonnie relied on the kindness of her co-workers to help her through the transition and rarely opened the practice software.

Suddenly, the day came when the system went live, and Bonnie found herself unprepared. Some of her co-workers were off that day, and she felt uncomfortable asking her manager for help, since she feared at least a stern reprimand for not being prepared.

Bonnie's manager was truly frustrated. He had tried to encourage Bonnie to get familiar with the system, even scheduling time away from circulation duties, and then saw Bonnie unwilling to use the time. While he felt there might be some learning style issues to be faced in Bonnie's case, he felt there also might be more than a good dose of stubbornness involved. He now had a circulation clerk who could not function, and patrons who were less willing to be kind and forgiving.

Case study analysis

Nicol Lewis

It is recommended that Bonnie's manager arrange a meeting both to discuss her developmental needs and to present goals that she must achieve over the course of a 30-day probationary period.

As outlined in the case study, the 'Sommerville library system gave everyone a few months to learn the ropes in practice mode before going live' and Bonnie was 'repeatedly offered quiet practice time at an office computer away from the circulation desk.' This resulted in no improvements in Bonnie's work ethic or performance. Further, it was visibly affecting her morale and would likely affect the morale of her colleagues who have been holding her weight.

The following approach is recommended to Bonnie's manager in remedying the situation:

- First, Bonnie should review the lessons provided in her training in her own time and not the library's. This includes the circulation training packet and the software available on a system available to library patrons.

- Secondly, while Bonnie is learning the system, the manager should allow Bonnie to shadow a colleague who has mastered the system for one week to obtain 'hands-on' training with the new system. During the second week, Bonnie will work unassisted – more familiarity with the system should increase her confidence and comfort level with operating the system independently.

- Thirdly, Bonnie will no longer be able to answer the phones or handle any other menial administrative activities until she has mastered the duties outlined in her job description. Instead, she will be required to increase her interaction with library patrons to improve her customer service and problem-solving skills.

- Finally, at the close of Bonnie's 30-day probationary period, the manager should evaluate her performance to determine if Bonnie will be able to continue in her current role or have her employment terminated.

Alternative scenarios

Write an analysis of the case study as it is presented or develop a scenario and suggest a possible solution. This can be a group activity.

Discussion questions

1. What are the real issues in this case?

2. How would you resolve these issues with Bonnie if you were the branch manager?

Conclusion

Ravonne A. Green

We have all heard it said that you do not learn everything in library school. As professionals, we deal with problems and situations that require using critical thinking and effective decision-making skills. The case study approach helps us to develop effective lifelong problem-solving skills.

Robert Stake (1995) writes about developing case studies for instructive purposes as an art. Learning this art as a library professional helps us to consider problems globally, seeing the whole picture instead of just the small segments that tend to affect us most. When we practise the art of case studies, we tend to enable those around us to consider aspects of the total view instead of focusing on minute details that lead to minimalization and ultimately to dysfunctionality. We consider policies, personalities, procedures, precedents, reactions, and consequences instead of isolated incidents.

Knowles (1975), in describing andragogy theory, emphasizes that adults are self-directed and take responsibility for decisions. Andragogy makes the following assumptions about the design of learning: (1) adults need to know why they need to learn something; (2) adults need to learn experientially; (3) adults approach learning as problem-solving; and (4) adults learn best when the topic is of immediate value (Faires, 2006).

In practical terms, andragogy means that instruction for adults needs to focus more on the process and less on the content being taught. Strategies such as case studies, role playing, simulations, and self-evaluation are most useful. Library directors and instructors adopt a role of facilitator or resource rather than lecturer or sage on the stage.

While each case is unique, cases tend to have a universal quality. Cases included in the library literature and from other sources can easily be adapted for the local setting for instruction purposes. Case studies are useful as tools for personnel evaluation. Case studies can be used as an objective means for handling problems with an individual or department. Case studies are a good training tool for disability awareness or diversity issues. Case studies provide a meaningful forum for program planning and evaluation. Case studies are particularly useful for program evaluation with all of the stakeholders contributing data, narrative comments, and suggestions for improvement.

- *Chapter 3: Utilizing the case study approach for program evaluation.* The consultant for this case study will need to consult with all of the key stakeholders before signing a contract and making a commitment to South Central University. The library, the library staff, and university administrators will be committing to a strenuous course of action. The costs in terms of time, human resources, and materials will be great. The case study researcher cannot afford to make costly errors.

- *Chapter 4: Special funding: use it or lose it.* This is an example of an instrumental case study. We learn about the significance of case studies for program management in discussing this case study. Ms Flannigan was forced to work through some difficult decisions that would ultimately involve careful program management.

- *Chapter 5: Employee training.* This is an example of a particularistic case study. This case study involves training and advancement opportunities for one individual and the particular decisions that she makes. Even though this case study involves one individual, the particular elements of this case are universal and can be used to teach universal principles that are related to the case.

- *Chapter 6: Censorship issues.* This is an example of an instrumental case study. While it focuses on a particular library and its dilemma over the decision to purchase an R-rated movie, the purpose is to focus on the policy issues related to this case. Policies are more general.

- *Chapter 7: Hiring decisions.* This is a particularistic case study. The focus is clearly on dealing with an employee that is displeased about a hiring decision. Like the case study in Chapter 5, this case may be applied to similar hiring situations in a more general context.

- *Chapter 8: To terminate or not to terminate, that is the question.* This is primarily a particularistic case study. However, it could be used as an instrumental case study because it clearly deals with policy issues.

- *Chapter 9: Privacy issues.* This is another instrumental case study. The issues and policies that this case addresses will have universal appeal.

- *Chapter 10: A question of service.* This focuses on a particular individual but the greater focus in studying this case study should be on policy and management issues.

- *Chapter 11: Here's the new library, where are the staff?* This is an instrumental, problem-solving case. The library

director who wears many other hats needs to address
management issues based on sound documentation from
professional organizations, benchmarking data, and
university and state policies to clearly state her case for
additional staff. She needs to request an appropriate job
description that matches her duties.

- *Chapter 12: Can you teach an old dog new tricks?* This
  case study is a particularistic case study but may also be
  instrumental in demonstrating the universal need for
  documenting employee training effectiveness. Many
  libraries have spent thousands of dollars sending
  employees to various training sessions only to learn that
  certain individuals have not been trained for the intended
  tasks. This case shows the importance of regular follow-
  up and regulated practice after training opportunities
  have been presented.

References and further reading

Faires, D. (2006) 'San Jose State University Blackboard
Training Module.' Unpublished.

Knowles, M. (1975) *Self-Directed Learning*. Chicago:
Follet.

Knowles, M. (1984a) *The Adult Learner: A Neglected
Species*, 3rd edn, Houston, TX: Gulf.

Knowles, M. (1984b) *Andragogy in Action*. San Francisco:
Jossey-Bass.

Stake, R. (1995) *The Art of Case Study*. Thousand Oaks,
CA: Sage.

Case study resources

- *http://web.cba.neu.edu/~ewertheim/introd/cases.htm*
- *http://bingweb.binghamton.edu/~tchandy/Mgmt411/ case_guide.html*
- *http://writecenter.cgu.edu/students/buscase.html*
- *http://choo.fis.utoronto.ca/FIS/Courses/LIS1230/ LIS1230sharma/history1.htm*

–

Index

analytical induction, 29, 44
axial coding, 44

bounded case, 11
bounded system, 11

case context, 57, 60
case definition, 17, 57
case expectations, 17, 57,
    60
case-oriented analysis, 44,
    57
causal patterns,10
chain sampling, 29
    see also snowball
    sampling
coding, 43–4, 49, 57
collective case studies, 13,
    17
conceptual framework, 37,
    45, 58–9
confirming cases, 32–3
constant comparative
    method, 43
content analysis, 54, 57

convenience sampling, 36–7
criterion sampling, 30
critical case sampling, 28
critical cases, 25, 28–9, 59
cross-analyze, 26
cross-case analysis, 15–17,
    42–3
cumulative epiphanies, 14

data analysis, 44, 55, 57,
    61, 79
data sources, 16–17
deviant case sampling, 25
    see also extreme cases
disconfirming cases, 32–3
    see also confirming cases
document analysis, 11

embedded analysis, 16, 18
epiphany, 14
exemplary case, 38
exploratory interviews, 39,
    57
extreme cases, 25, 59

foreshadowing, 40, 58

generalizability, 12, 38, 43
ground, 38
grounded theory, 43–5,
    57–8, 61, 63
grounding, 5, 11

heuristic research, 26
holistic, 16–18, 30
holistic analysis, 16–17
homogeneous samples, 27
hypotheses, 5, 37, 39

in vivo codes, 43
instrumental, 13, 15–16, 18,
    24, 38–9, 65, 154–5
instrumentation, 38, 58
intensity sampling, 24
interpretations, 41, 58
interviews, 9, 11, 17, 23,
    25, 31, 33, 35–6, 39,
    46, 52–4, 57, 59, 70–1,
    109–10
investigating, 40, 58, 137,
    139

maximum variation
    sampling, 26–8
mixed methodologies, 42
multi-site study, 11
multiple case design, 45
multiple case studies, 37,
    55

multiple comparison groups,
    45–6, 57–8
multiple exemplars, 45,
    47–8, 57–8
multiple operationalism,
    31
multiple-case data, 43, 58

naturalistic generalizations,
    13

observation, 11, 17–18, 28,
    32, 33, 38–42, 49–52,
    54, 56–9
open coding, 43
opportunistic sampling,
    33

particularistic, 13–15, 18,
    42, 49, 169–70
    see also intrinsic
politically important cases,
    36
probability sampling, 25, 59
problem definition, 24
purposeful random
    sampling, 36
purposeful sampling, 25, 28,
    37, 59

quantitative content
    analysis, 54
questionnaires, 11, 35–6,
    46

replication construct, 46
replication strategy, 44–5,
   57–8
reporting strategies, 16, 18
reporting timelines, 18
research questions, 16, 31,
   37–40, 58–60

sample, 9, 25, 27, 31, 35–6,
   59
sampling, 25–31, 33–7, 45,
   59–60
sampling types, 25
snowball sampling, 30
   see also chain sampling
stakeholders, 18–19, 24, 51,
   53, 57, 59, 68, 154
stratified purposeful
   sampling, 28
structured interview, 51, 53,
   59

structured observations,
   50–1, 59

theoretical replication,
   45
triangulation, 12, 37, 70
typical case sampling, 27
typical cases, 25, 27, 59

unstructured interviews, 53,
   59
unstructured observations,
   51

validity, 12, 38, 42
variable-oriented analysis,
   48, 59
varied cases, 25, 59

within-case analysis, 19
within-site study, 11

Printed in the United States
108918LV00001B/46/A

7520